BUT FIRST, COFFEE

BUT FIRST, COFFEE

A Guide to Brewing from the Kitchen to the Bar

Jordan Michelman and Zachary Carlsen

UNION
SQUARE
& CO.

NEW YORK

UNION SQUARE & CO.
SQUARE
& CO.
NEW YORK

UNION SQUARE & CO. and the distinctive Union
Square & Co. logo are registered trademarks of
Sterling Publishing Co., Inc.

Union Square & Co., LLC, is a subsidiary of
Sterling Publishing Co., Inc.

Text © 2023 Jordan Michelman and Zachary Carlsen

ISBN 978-1-4549-4769-1 (hardcover)
ISBN 978-1-4549-4770-7 (e-book)

Library of Congress Control Number: 2023932681

For information about custom editions, special
sales, and premium purchases, please contact
specialsales@unionsquareandco.com.

Printed in China

2 4 6 8 10 9 7 5 3 1

unionsquareandco.com

Editor: Caitlin Leffel
Designer: Ian Dingman with Christine Heun
Interior and Back Cover Photography:
  © 2023 Zachary Carlsen
Front Cover Photography: Sarah Jun,
  © 2023 Union Square & Co., LLC
Cover Food Styling: Jesse Szewczyk
Director of Photography: Jennifer Halper
Creative Director: Melissa Farris
Production Manager: Kevin Iwano
Production Editor: Christina Stambaugh
Copy Editors: Kathy Brock and Elizabeth Smith
Proofreaders: Diana Drew and Hope Clarke
Indexer: Elizabeth Parson

For Sara and Ross.

Contents

Welcome to But First, Coffee

The world is changing, and with it, so is the way we enjoy coffee.
Now more than ever, coffee lovers around the world are becoming home baristas, perfecting the art of the brew and making home coffee better.

Imagine for a moment that you're holding in your hands a beautiful bag of roasted coffee. Perhaps you've been given this as a gift, or you purchased it from your favorite espresso bar. Or maybe you bought it online from a roaster in a faraway city you love. Now that you're in possession of this wonderful roasted coffee product, what's your next move? Where do you go from here?

Turns out you're holding much more than a bag of coffee. In your hands is a passport, a history lesson, a portal to other cultures and traditions, and a ticket to a flight around the world. The bag of beans you now possess is ready to be put to delicious use, from the home coffee bar to the kitchen to the cocktail cart. One bag of coffee can be deployed in dozens of ways, throughout all hours of the day, yielding often surprising and delicious results.

We invite you to embrace these possibilities. Moreover, as an agricultural product capable of wildly diverse flavor experiences, coffee itself invites you. Once you accept that coffee is not *just* coffee but rather a thousand little choices leading up to unique expressions, coffee emerges as the main ingredient in a wider form of culinary and cultural application. Think of coffee more like flour, more like butter, more like water: a base element that can be manipulated and crafted in never-ending ways, depending on who you are and what you like.

First and foremost, there is the art of the brew. Brewing coffee for yourself and those you love is one of life's great pleasures, a sensory symphony of flavors. We fall asleep dreaming about the nice pot of coffee we'll brew first thing in the morning, but of course there are more esoteric brew methods for us to consider together. We've collected some of our favorites and will give you our tips and tricks for success at home. Coffee brewing can sometimes feel like laboratory science, but there's no need to feel intimidated. Self-expression is the goal here, and at its very best, the art and science of coffee brewing makes us *feel* something meaningful. A cup of coffee is delicious, but it's also much, much more than that.

POURING LATTE ART.

But brewing is just the beginning. Considering once more the bag of coffee in your hands, we want to appreciate this beautiful product first and foremost as an ingredient, ready to be deployed in myriad interesting ways across your kitchen. Coffee has a long history of intertwining with a diverse coterie of culinary pursuits, from the stovetop to the fridge to the baking tray. Let's embrace it, exploring and experimenting with the culinary potential of coffee with utterly tasty results.

All this coffee talk has us thirsty, which means soon it'll be the perfect time for a considered coffee cocktail. There are many parallels between coffee making and cocktail crafting, and so we've whipped up some of our favorite traditional coffee cocktails, developed intriguing zero-proof riffs for a few iconic drinks, and created a few original coffee cocktails of our own (after much delightful trial and error).

All this from one little bag of beans? It's possible! More than ever, coffee lovers are drinking coffee at home, but that shouldn't feel intimidating. Coffee drinking at home can be delicious, and, moreover, it should be fun. That's the goal of this book—to arm readers with the knowledge and insight needed to bring joy and light to the home coffee-making process for everyone.

The Voices in This Book

When we (Jordan and Zachary) cofounded Sprudge.com in 2009, coffee culture in the United States looked a lot different than it does today. The movement around a new sort of coffee culture, which is sometimes called "specialty coffee" or "third wave coffee," was still pretty small; back then you could count the number of these types of cafes in a place like Los Angeles or New York City on one hand. That is not the case today: cool coffee shops have become an expected urban amenity and are increasingly found in medium- and small-size cities in every corner of the United States.

In the early days, people used to ask us, "Can you really publish a website that's *just* about coffee?" We don't get asked that question anymore—instead we get asked for great cafe recommendations and for tips on how to make killer coffee at home.

Along the way, over the last decade we've come to know some pretty smart and extraordinary people who are experts in the coffee field. Their work has inspired us; visiting their cafes, drinking the coffee they grow on their farms, and listening to their ideas about coffee have helped us think more deeply about a beverage we love so much. And so that's why throughout this book you'll be hearing from a few of the smartest coffee people we know, offering helpful hints and tips along the way. Their voices contribute to how we think about coffee, and we want to pass along their insights to you as readers.

The one idea repeatedly invoked by every single person we spoke to is perhaps the simplest: have fun with your coffee. Making coffee at home is so immensely rewarding. In the pages to come, we'll do our best to arm you with things like suggested brewing ratios, temperatures, and techniques, but at every step of the way, we want you to remember that none of this is dogma. Listen to us, but not too hard. And keep the voices of our friends in mind throughout—their knowledge and expertise can guide us all.

Part 1

BREWING AT HOME: GETTING STARTED

Chapter 1

A BEGINNER'S APPROACH

Let's get something out of the way right now: it's quite likely that you, reading this book, are familiar with the beloved beverage coffee. Perhaps you've been making coffee for yourself each morning (and sometimes in the afternoon!) almost every day of your life, for years and years, even decades. But we do think there's something refreshing—humbling, even—about assuming a beginner's approach and considering the curatorial practice of coffee making at home with fresh eyes.

The truth is you need only a few things to make great coffee at home. That knowledge can be quite liberating. Over the years a great intellectual wall has been built up around coffee making, convincing you that your home setup must look like a scientific laboratory, beakers and burners splayed out across your countertop, kettles akimbo, all of the measurements bafflingly tracked to the milliliter.

Allow us to put the kibosh on this notion right now. A beginner's approach can serve you well! No matter how knowledgeable you might be about coffee, considering the discipline with fresh eyes yields delicious results. And, above all else, coffee brewing should be fun, expressive, and (once you get the hang of it) surprisingly intuitive. Your home coffee ritual is more a matter of preference and individuality than a rote recitation of recipes and instructions; there should be some soul to it, and some feeling, which you'll see us advocate for again and again in the pages to come. Coffee is both science *and* art, and it can become like a form of self-expression once you've got the building blocks in place.

To start from scratch, here's all you really need:

⚡ **Delicious coffee**—a matter of taste, style, and proximity.

⚡ **A way to grind that coffee**—whether ground for you at the point of purchase or by using a home grinder, one must transform the whole bean into ground coffee before it can be brewed.

⚡ **Water**—the introduction of water over ground coffee is what produces the "coffee" beverage we know and love.

⚡ **A brew method**—the apparatus through which water meets ground coffee.

⚡ **A measuring implement**—this can be as simple as a coffee scoop or as refined as a specialized digital scale that measures down to 0.1 gram.

For what it's worth, we feel strongly about the benefits of using a scale for precision when measuring your coffee—more on that on page 40.

That's it! Five things, albeit with endless variation and tweakability. Let's proceed from here together and dial your home coffee brewing in a bit.

"I always want my coffee to taste good, so to me, it's worth sometimes pouring out a coffee if it doesn't quite taste right. I like to be able to restart the process and make it a little bit better. This is a great way for me to start my day, with a little win. If I get it right the first time, that's a win, or the second time, that's a win, too. Ultimately, for me, coffee is the greatest gift I have to give to other people. The idea of hospitality—giving it to myself and allowing myself to reap the benefits of this skill I have—has opened me up for so much more general mindfulness and self-compassion."

—Bud Taliaferro, Austin, Texas, coffee educator and pop-up cafe manager

The Right Setup for You

Coffee brewing at home is endlessly personal and profoundly customizable, which is a great deal of fun for coffee lovers. It can be as simple as you'd like it to be or as complex as you'd dare to dream. For us, the best home-brewing method lies somewhere between the two: considered enough to produce a delicious cup but without *too* much fuss and artifice. You need something that will fire you up in the morning and deliver a dose of much-needed pep. It should be both delicious *and* easy, and this happy confluence is eminently possible.

Using the five elements of brewing on page 3, here are a few possible ways they could look in practice:

Incredibly Easy: Buy coffee from your local roaster and ask them to grind it for you. Use an automatic brewer (more on those in the next section) and follow the machine's instructions for amounts of coffee and water. Hit a button once that's done and voilà—the coffee is ready.

Still Very Easy: Buy coffee from your local roaster but grind it yourself at home using a home burr grinder (see page 11). Quickly weigh out the appropriate amount of coffee, then grind it on demand before adding it to your coffee machine. Hit a button and you're done—this coffee might be a touch fresher and slightly more delicious than using pre-ground beans, and the whirr of your coffee grinder will become a symphony to the ears each morning.

Intermediate: Buy coffee from your local roaster and grind it yourself. Weigh out the appropriate amount of coffee and water, then hand-brew that coffee using the brewing implement of your choice. Be sure to carefully measure the amount of coffee and water you're using and set a brewing timer. This is a bit more complex than using an automatic brewer, but it's also more personal and ritualistic. The coffee you make for yourself with this method isn't necessarily "better" than that using an automatic machine, but the extra step of hand-brewing is, for so many coffee lovers, a profoundly pleasurable experience.

Advanced: Buy green coffee from a notable importer, roast it yourself using a home coffee roaster, then meticulously rest, grind, and weigh the coffee before adding it to an elaborate grinding and brewing system that takes up much of your available kitchen space. Dial this in again and again before you can achieve a coffee that meets your exacting standard, perhaps while reading Ovid's *Metamorphoses* (in the original Latin, of course).

We're *mostly* joking about the last one; you wouldn't believe some of the home coffee setups we've encountered in the course of publishing Sprudge. The method we like using at home is the "still very easy" category: a home coffee-making machine paired with freshly ground coffee. Allow us to explain a bit more about why we love this approach.

An Appreciation of Automatic Coffee Makers

We could write lavish stanzas, entire sonnets about our vigorous appreciation of and daily devotion to the modern home coffee maker. These trusty units have come a long way from the days of the hotel room auto-pot, the dingy diner hot plate, and the stinky junk shop percolator. Today's market for automatic coffee makers is modern and inspiring, with options that are sure to look great on your countertop and capable of making delicious coffee morning after morning, with results every bit as good as what's on the filter bar at your favorite cafe, thanks to temperature-stable electronics and heat-stable carafes.

We love the home automatic coffee maker for its dependability and ease of use; yes, even professional coffee geeks like us have learned to trust and appreciate the joyous simplicity of an automatic coffee maker in the home. There's something charming and intuitive about the whole process: add ground coffee to machine, add water to machine, hit button, wait briefly, enjoy coffee. It allows the morning to proceed accordingly and provides piping-hot delicious coffee with just the touch of a button.

Still, there is some nuance at play. One is the grinder: we really do recommend employing a home grinder in your daily coffee regimen. The second is the water; depending on where you live in the world, your tap water might be perfect for coffee brewing, or it could be worthwhile to consider treating or outsourcing your water to the benefit of the finished brew (see page 14). And it also matters *which* coffee brewer you pick, a matter about and to which there is endless opinion and consideration. Here are automatic coffee makers we like and trust, starting with our favorite:

TECHNIVORM MOCCAMASTER AND SUAY CERAMICS MUG.

Technivorm Moccamaster: This has long been a house favorite for us at Sprudge—it's as sleek and stylish as it is easy to use and dependable. It comes with a thermal carafe, available in a pleasing array of colors, that keeps coffee hot and fresh for hours. The Moccamaster's minimalist Dutch design has become a classic in the coffee space, and we swear by the coffee that this brand of automatic coffee makers is capable of.

The OXO Brew: With a sturdy carafe and simple interface, the relatively new OXO Brew is simple to use but comes with more in the way of features than the Moccamaster. With some models of the OXO Brew, you can, for example, program a timer function to make you coffee in the morning upon rising or calculate exactly how long it's been since the last pot was made. The OXO Brew makes use of an automatic pre-infusion mode meant to mimic the art of hand-brewed coffee, and you can adjust the parameters to brew more or less coffee on demand. It's a great product.

Bonavita Connoisseur: A well-known brand name for coffee-loving consumers, Bonavita's Connoisseur model is definitely worth your consideration. It makes use of a flat-bottomed basket and is especially easy to use, thanks to easily understandable measurement directions printed on the machine itself. This is the least expensive of the home brewers we recommend, and over the years we've set up our friends and families with it as they explore the wonders of home automatic brewers.

With any of the above brewers—or any other home brewer on the market—a regular regimen of cleaning is not just advised, but required. Coffee is a wonderfully complex substance on a chemical scale, but that complexity means there's all manner of gunk and detritus left on your coffee machine after repeated use. Water is also complex—especially if you live in an area with hard water—and minerals will build up in your coffee maker. After each use you should wipe down your home coffee machine, but every 3 to 6 months it's time to deep clean and descale it. To do this, we favor a simple 1:1 ratio of hot water and white vinegar. Mix and pour this solution into the machine's water tank, then brew a pot as you would normally do if using coffee. Run one or two brews of clean water after using the vinegar solution to give the machine a good rinse and get rid of any leftover flavor. This will clean the guts out of your machine and improve flavor and brew stability, as well lengthen the lifetime of your coffee maker.

> "For me, my own personal coffee desire is all about the ritual of doing it first thing in the morning, because my life is really busy with kids and all the other things and I'm always the first one up. I make my coffee in my coffeepot and put the water in the night before. I even grind the night before so the grinder doesn't wake up the kids. That moment of being alone, the really quiet 10 minutes I get while the machine is brewing—I wouldn't trade that for anything. Having a few sips before everything goes crazy for the day is so important to me."
>
> **—Andrea Allen, Rogers, Arkansas, cofounder of Onyx Coffee Lab, and the 2020 United States Barista Champion**

The Grind Is Everything

For whatever reason—maybe because it's an extra expense, maybe because it seems kind of "fussy" or like too much trouble—a lot of daily coffee drinkers draw the line at purchasing a grinder for their home. We get it: not everyone needs the most deluxe version possible of their daily coffee habit. But for just about $100 or so for an electric unit, or as a low as $30 for a hand grinder, you can seriously up your home coffee game, improving the quality of your daily cup and opening up a world of possibilities.

We enthusiastically recommend grinding your own coffee fresh at home. Grinding at home is a rewarding experience: the expressive, volatile aromatics fill the room, and the freshly ground coffee comes alive with flavor. Pre-ground

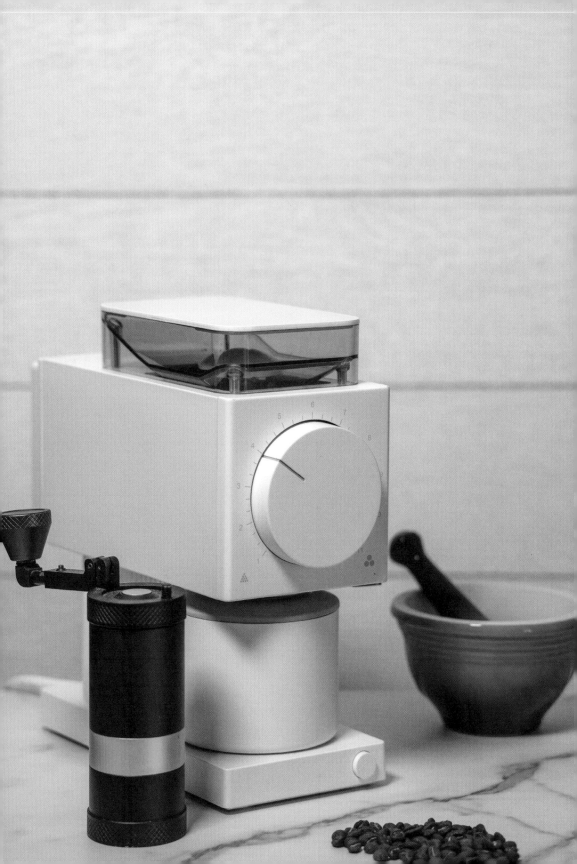

coffee works fine in a pinch, but over time the vibrancy of coffee begins to grow stale and fade. And in the pages to come, we'll be brewing, cooking, steeping, infusing, and cocktailing with freshly ground coffee.

The consistency of ground coffee is a crucial component of coffee brewing. For percolating brew methods, it controls how fast or slow water passes through the coffee grounds. Without getting too technical, what we're talking about here is known as "extraction"—that's a way of describing how hot water and ground coffee combine to produce the brewed drink we know and love. A grind that is too fine can result in a very long brew time, and that extended contact with the ground coffee can pull bitter and astringent qualities out of it. Conversely, a grind that is too coarse can result in a rushed contact time, resulting in a thin, watery cup.

It's likely you're familiar with the "blade grinder" style of electric grinder, in which a high-speed spinning blade chops up coffee in a scissor-cutting action. In a pinch, one of these blade grinders is fine for making coffee, but we much prefer the style known as a "burr grinder" for brewing coffee at home. Burr grinders make use of two revolving screwlike surfaces that can be adjusted for distance. This allows the user to make the ground coffee coarser or finer, resulting in uniformly sized grind particles that help promote even extraction

OPPOSITE, FROM LEFT TO RIGHT: VSSL HAND GRINDER, FELLOW ODE GRINDER, LE CREUSET MORTAR AND PESTLE. ABOVE: COFFEE GROUND WITH A BLADE GRINDER (LEFT) AND COFFEE GROUND WITH A BURR GRINDER (RIGHT).

during the coffee-brewing process. A high-quality grinder with a machined burr set helps to yield a consistent, repeatable grind. Inexpensive grinders made with blades often yield a range of grind particle sizes—coarse and fine mingling together—resulting in a dissonant blend of ground coffee that water either gushes through or seeps through, creating a cup that's both somehow overextracted and underextracted at the same time.

Kindly trust us when we say that a burr grinder is really the best bet for your home coffee needs. Some of the brands we like include Baratza and Bonavita for electric units (starting at around $100) and Hario for a hand grinder (starting at around $30). Electric burr grinders plug right into the wall and operate at the push of a button. Hand burr grinders require you to physically crank the burrs using a handle, which can be kind of a pain and takes a little extra time, but it's also quite satisfying (and good for your arm muscles). And when it comes to espresso, having a high-quality grinder paired to your espresso machine is all but required. Some home espresso grinders we like are made by brands like Mahlkönig, Mazzer, and the aforementioned Baratza, and their price can range into the thousands of dollars.

"I use the combination of a hand grinder and a Kalita Wave when I travel to coffee origin countries and meet with coffee farmers. One of my favorite things to do is make the coffee that a producer grew for them to try—we'll do this together right there on the farm. A two-part setup like this is actually very convenient, and sometimes I find that a coffee grower may never have tasted their coffee before in this way. It allows us to share something bigger than coffee and to become friends. Having a travel setup like this makes me look forward to traveling that much more, and I've done this now with coffee producers from Panama to Colombia to Nicaragua and El Salvador."

—Freda Yuan, London, England, coffee educator, green coffee buyer, and author

How can you tell if your coffee grind is set? There are a few easy ways to determine whether your grind is too coarse or too fine.

⚡ Do you notice the water draws down too quickly, and your coffee is thin, grassy, or sour? Those are good signs that your grind is too coarse.

⚡ Does the water take a long time to draw down, and your coffee tastes bitter and acrid? It's too fine, and that coffee is over-extracted. Ideally your coffee brew times will match the brew times in this book, and one of the best ways to control that is with the grind.

The good news is that dialing in a grinder is rather straightforward, once you find that sweet spot—not too coarse, not too fine—for your brew method and volume. But that's not to say you won't want to make slight adjustments to your grind over time. Coffee is not all the same, and coffee varietals and processing methods result in individual coffees, each with its own set of differing densities. Climate and humidity can also affect a brew, so you'll want to keep an eye on your grind size as these variables change. Very little about coffee brewing is truly "set and forget"; think about this as a form of mindfulness, and enjoy checking in on your grinder often to make sure things are still happening the right way.

We use terminology like "sandbox sand" for particle size, but you can get quite, literally, granular with grind; many new grinders offer micro-adjustments for those who really want to nail the perfect brew. There is perhaps no variable

GROUND COFFEE (LEFT TO RIGHT): COARSE, MEDIUM, FINE.

SIDE-BY-SIDE COMPARISON OF GROUND COFFEE WITH A BURR GRINDER (LEFT) AND GROUND COFFEE WITH A BLADE GRINDER (RIGHT).

in all of home coffee brewing more infinitely adjustable than your grinder settings, but it's also possible to reach a sort of "analysis paralysis"—it's fun to focus on this stuff, but most of us don't need to focus *that* much. A solid grind profile on a grinder that has been regularly cleaned and mindfully adjusted is all you really need to strive for. With proper care and maintenance, a high-quality grinder can last a lifetime, and many reputable grinder companies offer generous warranties and customer service to keep your workhorse in tip-top shape.

Water for Coffee Brewing

Water, water everywhere but not a drop to . . . brew with?

A cup of coffee is more than 98 percent water, and good water is crucial for a proper extraction. If you're lucky enough to live in a city that has clean, odorless drinking water, then you probably already have the right stuff to brew a good cup of coffee.

If the tap water makes your hair weird, leaves a film on the shower curtain, or causes a quick buildup of scale on your home coffee maker, chances are the total dissolved solids (TDS) in your tap water are ill-suited to coffee brewing. Cities like Los Angeles are notorious for their high-TDS tap water, as opposed to places like New York City, Portland, and Seattle, whose water treatment is suited for optimal coffee brewing.

If you live somewhere with less-than-ideal tap water, consider modifying the water you brew coffee with. At the basic end of things, water filtered through a Brita or BWT filter will improve your brewing. As you get more into coffee brewing, consider investing in a higher-end water filter, or ask your local cafe about using some of their brewing water.

Water is a paradox when it comes to coffee: its role in how we brew coffee is tremendously important, and yet most people draw the line at water modification when it comes to their own home coffee-brewing situation. We get it: you're not running a science lab. But as a baseline, make the effort to use filtered water for your coffee brewing. Top-level cafes take water quality quite seriously, and this is one of the single biggest reasons why most coffee brewed at a cafe is often objectively better than most coffee brewed at home. If you're trying to slay the dragon of making cafe-quality coffee at home, water needs to be part of the conversation.

BREW TIP: Use filtered water when brewing your coffee, from a brand like Brita or BWT.

> "We dial in our water daily at Go Get Em Tiger, which I think is essential for making great coffee—especially somewhere like Los Angeles, where the water quality out of the tap isn't great. When I think about what's really important when it comes to coffee brewing, the whole bean coffee you buy is number one, but number two is the water—for me, this is way ahead of the technique and equipment. The water is the second most important factor in the outcome of what you're brewing, and I don't think most people understand that."
>
> **—Kyle Glanville, Los Angeles, California, founder of Go Get Em Tiger and the 2008 United States Barista Champion**

On-Demand Coffee's New Appraisal

In this section of the book, we've discussed a few different pathways for making coffee at home, with special attention given to the ease of use and reliability of a fine home automatic coffee maker. In the next chapter, we'll discuss hand-brewed coffee methods, with recipes that arm you for success each morning (and then again at 11 a.m. for the all-important midmorning cup). But before we move on, we'd be remiss not to discuss a particularly interesting development that's come to the fore in coffee over the last few years: the resurgence of on-demand coffee.

To be clear, we're using the term "on-demand" to refer to a broad spectrum of coffee delivery systems, including capsule systems, coffee pods, frozen concentrate, and powdered instant coffee. There's a stirring simplicity to be found in the use of these products, which is part of why they're so popular—the global market for coffee pods is north of $13 billion annually, and by some estimates, it will continue to grow by 5 percent each year into the future.

When we started writing about coffee, all the way back in 2009, there was a clearly defined "us vs. them" dichotomy between the world of quality coffee and the world of the coffee pods. But today this wall has been well and truly breached, with many of the coffee world's best roasters happily partnering with on-demand products to get their roasts into the mugs of as many coffee lovers as possible.

We watch this market closely and have tasted and enjoyed many of its offerings. Few companies in the world have done a better job of merging coffee's status as a gourmet beverage with the ease and convenience of an on-demand system like Nespresso, and, for what it's worth, we always stop into a Nespresso cafe when happening upon one during our travels. (They're usually located in the luxury part of town.) Back at home, brands like Blue Bottle Coffee (North America and Asia) and Colonna Coffee (United Kingdom and Europe) have helped establish the footing of on-demand coffee within the realm of contemporary, quality-focused coffee brands. Brands like Cometeer and Swift Coffee have brought instant and on-demand coffee into the specialty coffee zeitgeist, collaborating with multiple brands and widening the reach of coffee preparation in this style. (Which is why your favorite local roaster most likely now has an on-demand coffee offering available.)

Leaving aside the pods and pucks, we like quality instant coffee (such as that made by Joe Coffee of New York City)—and not just for drinking but for its wonderful utility across a broad range of culinary purposes. Later in this book are recipes for desserts, spice rubs, and cocktails that make ready use of fine specialty instant coffee, and so our advice is this: keep an open mind and grab a few packets of instant coffee the next time you order some beans. Let your embrace of the beginner's approach cross over into appreciating the modern coffee moment in all its forms—even instant. The rewards are ample.

Curating Your Mug Collection

There's one more aspect to our beginner's approach that's very much worth mentioning before we dive into the deep end of brew methods and variations: the mug you sip from once all that delicious coffee is ready. It might seem counterintuitive, but we are convinced that the coffee mug is no less important than any other step in the coffee-brewing process, albeit for reasons that reach beyond the temporal and more into the spiritual.

Our brains are the most marvelous things, fleshy supercomputers of remarkable complexity and precision, able to connect involuted concepts like "flavor" and "deliciousness" into something cohesive and memorable. But the flavor receptors in our tongue are also fallible and easily influenced by forces beyond proof of taste. Mellifluous music, a sweet evening breeze, charming company—all these forces can and do make things like food and wine taste better, to say nothing of artisan serving plates, antique flatware, a crisp white tablecloth, and any of the other restaurant tricks used to create an overall dining experience.

So it goes with coffee—our brains are influenced by everything around us at the moment of consumption. This means that when it comes time to pick a mug, the vessel you drink from matters a great deal. It can help the coffee taste better, creating a flavoristic experience with multiple dimensions and resonances. No coffee love can be truly satisfied by one mug alone. We've thought about this a great deal because we're mug lovers in a deep and

abiding way, collectors of many a mug from our years of travel and study across the world of coffee. Consider these earnest suggestions for choosing a marvelous mug, and trust us: this one weird trick will help deepen your appreciation of coffee in your home.

⚡ **Harness nostalgia:** A vintage mug emblazoned with your favorite cartoon character from childhood or a particularly memorable campaign from a beloved sports team can make for very happy drinking.

⚡ **Practice radical self-care:** Research has shown that just looking at positive affirmations can improve mental alertness, clarity, and mood—and that's before your first sip!

⚡ **Support ceramicists:** Coffee and the ceramic arts have long been fruitful bosom buddies. Chances are there's an artisan ceramist in your area making beautiful mugs for purchase. This is indeed a worthy investment.

⚡ **Bring your favorite cafe home:** Have you noticed that coffee just seems to taste better at your favorite diner or coffee shop? Many cafes sell the mugs they use for service, often displayed in a small selection of merchandise alongside things like whole bean coffee and tote bags. Or if it's the perfect diner mug you're after, check the bottom of the mug at your local coffee shop (once the coffee's been drunk, of course), and take note of the make and model for further inquiry.

A CABINET OF COLORFUL MUGS. TOP TO BOTTOM, LEFT TO RIGHT: CLAY PIG CERAMICS, WORN PATH, VINTAGE OWL, BEN MEDANSKY, JESS FAULK CERAMICS, KINTO, CLAY PIG CERAMICS, BEN MEDANSKY CERAMICS, JESS FAULK CERAMICS.

Chapter 2

DEEPER DOWN THE RABBIT HOLE

For many, making delicious coffee at home is a matter of convenience and repeatability, an avenue to provide the caffeinated fuel required to inspire everything else you've got going on in your life. There is no shame or "second-best" inherent to this outlook, and we've provided a working blueprint for this unfussy approach in chapter 1. But making coffee at home can also be a passion, a hobby, an endless, joyful equation comprising disparate variables, where every choice leads to another set of choices. As a daily practice, you come to realize that making coffee at home has no end point, no "perfect" solution, because it involves tapping into an operating system that's bigger than any one moment. Once you accept this, it becomes a form of meditation, and we can go deeper together down the path of coffee brewing as a hobby and passion. We can explore coffee not just as a beverage but as an agricultural product with its own unique set of intricacies related to crop cultivation, processing techniques, and global trade impact. From this point, there will always be tweaking, always refining, forever playing with a new roast or new coffee processing method or new brewer or new recipe.

What matters most is that you love it. Once this is established, a boundless sense of play and discovery is possible. In the pages to come, we offer a set of baseline suggestions for individual brewing methods, based on our own experience using them to brew coffee at home and in cafes. And we've also reached out to a couple of select experts for their own takes on brew methods and how they express themselves culturally and as individuals within the context of coffee appreciation. More than anything, we want to arm you with the knowledge and confidence to experiment with your own approach to making coffee at home. There is no single right way, no perfect ratio, no one mode above all else, and that's one reason we love coffee so much. It is a joyful rabbit hole.

Arabica vs. Robusta

Just about every coffee lover is familiar with the phrase "100% arabica coffee," which has been used with great effectiveness in coffee marketing efforts for decades, especially around the smooth, easy-drinking coffees of Colombia or your favorite latte at Starbucks. And conversely, we'd wager that quite a few of you are also familiar with the undeniable oomph of a shot of Italian espresso, whether you enjoyed it on a trip to Italy or at a coffee shop somewhere else in the world, oftentimes fortified with robusta beans.

Arabica and robusta are two different species of the coffee plant that have avowed followings worldwide. We use the word "coffee" to refer to both arabica and robusta, and they each have their own formal taxonomic name: *Coffea arabica* (arabica) and *Coffea canephora* (robusta). The plants actually look different, and they grow differently. Let's learn a bit more about them both as a helpful way of dialing in your coffee knowledge on the journey to home-brewing joy.

ARABICA COFFEE

⚡ **Sweet. Fragrant. Flavorful. These are words that come to** mind when we think of arabica coffee, which has formed the backbone of a modern appreciation of coffee. Some 60 percent of the coffee grown in the world is arabica, from the drip coffee on tap at your favorite coffee shop to the most prized and expensive micro lots.

⚡ **Arabica originated in Ethiopia centuries ago and today** grows in dozens of unique varieties sometimes termed as "heirloom." Within the wider world of arabica, there are several popular varieties and subvarieties found around the world, including Typica, Bourbon, Caturra, Gesha, Tekisic, and Pacamara, to name just a few. Each of these has its own unique flavor characteristics, interaction with soil terroir and elevation, which create distinct, memorable coffees.

⚡ **Arabica can be absolutely delicious, but it is also fussy,** susceptible to disease and crop failure. For this reason, an over-reliance on arabica has placed coffee farmers in a precarious position, particularly in the face of climate change. Many coffee experts today are looking for ways to hybridize arabica to produce coffee plants that are delicious *and* stable enough to meet modern challenges.

ROBUSTA COFFEE

⚡ **Bold. Strong. Powerful. These are some of the terms** commonly associated with robusta coffee, which you might know from drinking a classic Italian-style shot of espresso. Around 40 percent of the coffee grown worldwide is robusta, and that number is on the rise, thanks to the crop's hearty nature and resistance to disease.

⚡ **Originating in sub-Saharan Africa, robusta coffee is widely** grown in countries including Uganda and the Democratic Republic of the Congo. Today it is also found on low-elevation farms in countries like Vietnam and Brazil, where a high volume of robusta coffee is produced.

⚡ **Robusta is often blended with arabica, not only in the** classic Italian espresso but also in popular consumer brands like Café Bustelo and Folgers. Quality robusta is on the rise, and its higher caffeine content and low, round acidity make for a perfect foil to arabica's singing high notes—top with just a dollop of foam, as in a classic macchiato, and you've got the perfect Italian espresso experience.

Proof of Taste: Natural vs. Washed

Before we zoom in on brewing methods, let's address one of the most important parts of the coffee story that will ultimately impact your cup's flavor. We are referring to *coffee processing*, a big, imperfect term that requires some brief unpacking (and a pocket botany lesson).

Every cup of coffee you have ever enjoyed in your life started out as the fruit of a small tree, sometimes called a *shrub*, other times a *treelet*, depending on whom you ask. We rather like *treelet* as the most apt descriptor of the coffee plant, so let's go with that. The treelet has its genetic roots in Ethiopia, or maybe Yemen (again, depending on whom you ask), and it was distributed around the world as a cash crop to now-famous growing regions like Brazil, Colombia, Indonesia, and Kenya by way of colonialism.

No matter where coffee grows, when the fruit of the coffee treelet ripens—sometimes appearing red, sometimes yellow or orange—inside of it lies the marvelous coffee seed. Note we say *seed* and not *bean*; although we've all been calling them "coffee beans" our entire life, that's not entirely accurate. Some kind of action is required—a process—to remove the fruit of the coffee cherry from the seeds inside, and this process has a dramatic impact on the resulting coffee's flavor.

The two most common terms used in coffee to describe processing are *natural* and *washed*. Natural is the oldest method, so let's start there.

NATURAL PROCESS COFFEE

⚡ **The term *natural process* refers to what occurs when the** whole coffee fruit is left intact to dry after being harvested. To start, the coffee cherry is plucked from the treelet. Then it's set aside to dry in the sun, fruit and all.

⚡ **A combination of gravity and solar heat helps impart** natural flavors into the bean itself, and after about two weeks, the fruit has dried around the seeds and is ready to be removed. Sugar fermentation within the fruit occurs at this time, which is why natural process coffees can sometimes have a funky or musky flavor, not unlike certain natural wines or craft beers. Once the cherry has dried, it is milled manually or mechanically.

⚡ **Relying primarily on heat and gravity, the natural process** is the original form of coffee processing, and it's still most commonly used in parts of the world where access to water can be scarce, such as Ethiopia and Yemen. But it is a process employed in other parts of the world, including Brazil, Colombia, and Costa Rica, where farmers use it out of necessity or because they enjoy the ritual and flavor of this ancient practice.

⚡ **Natural process coffees can taste wild and evocative, with** deep, complex fruit flavors reminiscent of cherries and blueberries. Not everyone loves them, and there is some controversy in the coffee industry around these coffees, especially among longtime coffee professionals. But these coffees are uniquely capable of an "aha" moment related to the appreciation of coffee as a culinary pleasure. Nothing else tastes quite like a beautifully handled, intentionally brewed cup of natural process coffee.

WASHED PROCESS COFFEE

⚡ **A more recent invention than the natural process, the** washed process is believed to have started in Ethiopia and rose to popularity during the mid-nineteenth century in producing countries like Kenya and Colombia. The coffee cherry is de-pulped and the residual coffee fruit (mucilage) is removed by fermentation. It's then thoroughly washed and dried. Today, it is among the most popular methods of coffee processing for specialty coffee producers. It yields a well-defined cup of coffee, though it may not be as interesting or unique as natural processed coffees.

⚡ After a coffee cherry is picked, it goes to a special facility for coffee washing, which is sometimes referred to as a *washing station* or a *factory* (different names are used around the world). Sometimes these are modest, used by just a few farmers to wash their coffees, but other times—like at the Buf Café washing station in central Rwanda, which we visited in 2013—they are massive, taking up an entire hillside and bringing in coffee from dozens or even hundreds of individual farmers across the region.

⚡ There is considerable variation in how each washing station "washes" its coffee, but the process often looks something like this: First the coffee is floated in tanks of water, which helps to detect underripe cherries (which float to the top). Next, special machinery removes the cherry husk; from there, the seed is fermented in tanks for anywhere from half a day to several days, depending on the style of the washing station. Last, the washed coffee seeds are then dried in the sun on raised beds, on patios, or in mechanical dryers, and tended to regularly by workers at the washing station to ensure even drying and consistent moisture content.

⚡ Washed coffees can help produce clean, bright flavors in the cup, with red apple acidity and pleasant notes of stone fruit. This method requires more water to process coffee and has been critiqued for being environmentally unsustainable. Washed coffees tend to be very popular among coffee lovers, and it's all but certain that your favorite coffee roaster will have several washed coffees to choose from for you to enjoy.

⚡ These are the two main processing methods, but they are not the *only* processing methods. The farther down the rabbit hole you go, the more likely you are to encounter fairly esoteric coffee processes including the honey process, a kind of hybrid of the washed and natural processes and named for the honey-like mucilage that clings to the coffee seed after the fruit is removed, as well as the anaerobic process, in which coffee is fermented without oxygen, and carbonic maceration, when the entire coffee cherry is added to the fermentation tank. And that's just the start: there is also the koji process, in which koji mold, more popularly known for its use in brewing Japanese sake, is added to coffee cherries, and the lactic process, in which lactic acid bacteria is used to remove the coffee fruit from the cherry.

⚡ **Most infamous is the practice known as _kopi luwak_, in** which the Indonesian palm civet (a sort of jungle weasel also known as a _luwak_) ingests coffee cherries whole, digests them by absorbing the coffee cherry fruit via its weasely stomach acid, and poops the seeds out. Their poop is then harvested for the seeds, which are washed, roasted, and sold for astronomically high prices. There are similar gimmicks we've heard of involving Brazilian jacu birds, elephants, and the coati, a raccoon-like mammal that lives in the jungles of Brazil and Central America. For some, trying coffee processed in one of these methods is a bucket-list moment, but we've never been fans—animal processing often involves force feeding, and the flavor compares poorly to the culinary possibilities of today's modern coffee-processing methods.

Importers and Exporters Are So Important

Now you know that the type of bean matters (arabica or robusta) and that the way coffee producers process the bean matters (washed or natural, usually). But what comes next? Once the coffee is processed, the next steps in the chain are of critical importance. At every step of the way, raw coffee must be treated with respect, as an artisan agricultural product capable of achieving the highest heights of delicious flavor.

Coffee uses an exporter-to-importer model similar to many other international goods. A network of exporters operates in every coffee-producing country in the world, procuring raw coffee (which is sometimes called "green" coffee) and distributing it for the international market. This looks a little different in every country: in Ethiopia, a nationalized system called the Ethiopian Commodity Exchange functions almost like the stock market, creating a centralized exchange system of sellers and buyers that move fine Ethiopian coffee from the farmers to the international market; in Colombia, independent exporters partner with small, quality-focused importers to market sought-after coffees.

Exporters work with importers in coffee-drinking countries, including the United States, to negotiate prices and manage the oftentimes difficult logistical work of physically getting raw coffee out of one country and into another one. Importers procure coffee, secure its safe travel, then take responsibility for receiving it once it arrives in the destination country. From there, importers work directly with roasters to provide samples of coffee, negotiate sales and distribution agreements, and create a reliable product flow. Importers are the last step in the chain before coffee arrives at the door of the roastery, but they are also important sources of education and relationship building between the roasters and the coffee farmers at origin.

It is perhaps tempting to look at this group—the exporters and importers—as a series of middlemen—people who are not directly involved in the farming or the roasting of the coffees we enjoy. But this is much too simple and, in our opinion, an inaccurate read of the situation. Coffee is grown by real people, and it is a raw, sometimes mercurial agricultural product that undertakes a long, difficult journey from the coffee farm to your local cafe. Without responsible exporters and importers, this work would be impossible.

Over the last few decades, the role of green coffee importers has grown considerably, and this (not coincidentally) dovetails with the ongoing explosion of quality coffee availability and coffee's growing esteem as a culinary delicacy. Many modern importers pride themselves not only on their product but also on their status as a knowledge hub and a way for roasters to be more directly connected to the artisan coffee farmers whose beans they roast. Roasters that want to develop relationships with coffee farmers often do so via connections created by the importers themselves, and importers are able to foster meaningful, ongoing, multiyear contractual relationships with coffee farmers, rewarding them for hard work and coffee quality.

You might not think about the importance of exporters and importers when you brew yourself a cup of something delicious, and that's fine. This part of the coffee process happens mostly out of sight for the average coffee drinker, but it remains vitally important all the same. Great coffee starts at the farm and ends in your cup, and along the way there are critical touch points that make it all possible. We think they deserve some celebration from time to time. After all, there is no great coffee without great exporters and importers.

Roasters Are Important, Too

The last step in the chain is one you might be more familiar with: the coffee roaster. This is the person who is responsible for selling you a bag of delicious coffee. However, before they can do that, the raw coffee must be finished, or "roasted," to create the coffee experience we all know and love.

Coffee roasting is both a science and an art, and dedicated roasters spend years—even decades—perfecting their approach, learning their gear, and honing their craft. In the olden days, much of coffee roasting was done by sight, sound, and timer; today there are state-of-the-art technological setups that help roasters dial in their roasts using sensors and software, tracking roast curves and creating repeatable profiles to ensure a stable finished product.

In our experience the best roasting is a fusion of these two approaches: the sensory aspect still matters, and a tuned-in roaster carefully watches every change in their roasting process, like a baker carefully tending to an oven or a barbecue pitmaster maintaining a fire. But the new era of technology arms them with tools to achieve even better results. There is a balanced contrast to this sort of work, and that's what we mean when we say roasting is both art and science.

For consumers, the most important part of a roast is known as a "roast level"—this is a way of saying how darkly roasted the beans get by the end of the process. "Darker" beans might appear a deep oxidized brown color, or even black, with an oily sheen, and in the cup this results in classically "bold" notes. This is sometimes referred to as "French roast," and this style of roasting has its lifelong devotees. In more recent years, a "lighter" approach to roasting has gone through a significant phase of popularity, inspired by the roasting traditions of Scandinavia, where coffee is typically roasted to a fawn-light brown. This results in a coffee that is tealike and some feel more expressive of the terroir and varietal characteristics of the coffee being roasted.

Most roasters favor a sort of middle ground between the two styles: not so roasted as to create burnt notes, but not so light as to be reminiscent of tea. This is sometimes called "medium roast," though a whole scale of roast terms (such as "full city," which indicates a darker roast) can be used to denote the subtle differences between a given roast of coffee. Some roasters offer a range of roast profiles to meet the preferences of their customers; others pride themselves on specializing in one specific style of roasting, be it light or dark.

Ultimately the style of roast you choose to brew coffee at home is a matter of preference, and there's no wrong way to enjoy coffee. In our opinion, the wide world of roast profiles is just more proof of coffee's vast array of possibilities and flavors, and we encourage you to experiment with different styles of roasted coffee. If you've been drinking French roast coffee black as the night for decades, you might be shocked at how interesting, flavorful, and fruity a cup of lightly roasted coffee can taste. Conversely, if you only purchase the lightest of the light roasts in the Scandinavian style, you'll be astonished at how delicious a deep, well-roasted cup of darker coffee can taste in the right roaster's hands. We tend to enjoy daily drinking coffees that walk the middle path: not too dark, not too light, just right.

As a last note, all this roasting talk may find you tempted to tackle the challenge of roasting coffee yourself at home. This can be a lot of fun, and it's definitely one more potential component of a home coffee hobby. Home roasting has ardent fans, and they're often some of the most knowledgeable and opinionated coffee drinkers around. For most people, it's not necessary to learn to roast coffee at home, but for some, it becomes a lifelong passion and point of pride. As for us? Well—we like to stick with the experts. There is no substitute for the decades of expertise, state-of-the-art gear, close relationships with importers, and focus on dependable quality at scale you get from an artisan roaster. There are so many wonderful roasters to choose from, and nowadays a new crop of subscription services is available to bring roasters from around the world to your doorstep. Each has a unique take not just on coffee but on packaging and branding, making for a sort of consumable art that is a joy to behold.

Buy Lots of Coffee from Different Roasters

We could never stop at just one roaster—life is too short, and coffee is too delicious. In the pages to come, you'll hear us talk about a couple of specific coffee roasting companies, often with specific pairings in

WHOLE BEAN COFFEE (TOP TO BOTTOM, LEFT TO RIGHT) FROM JOE COFFEE, FORE-CAST COFFEE, OLYMPIA COFFEE, PROUD MARY COFFEE, CASA BRASIL, METHODICAL.

> "For me, the unlock that brings me joy is the idea that multiple coffee companies can give you multiple avenues of joy and different forms of pleasure. It's not just having perfectly roasted Gesha or a cool blend; it's about more than what's in the cup. It's about identifying interesting people making coffee and being interested in their stories. It's an analog act, more like record collecting or something like that. I love sitting with different bags of coffee and feeling inspired by them."
>
> **—Matt Rodbard, New York, New York, coffee-loving editor, journalist, and author**

mind. Feel free to take our suggestions, but whatever you do, don't stop there. We are currently living in a golden age of coffee roasting: there has never been a better time to drink coffee as a consumer, and there's never been more quality-focused roasters to choose from in markets large and small, all around the world.

This means that as a coffee drinker, you are absolutely, completely, and truly spoiled for choice. If anything, it can be hard to know where to start, and that's okay—it's actually a fantastic problem to have. The odds are in your favor that you'll find a great roaster or two, or five or more, with coffee that you'll be happy to brew and tinker with at home.

The best place to start is your local coffee shop. Any coffee shop worth its salt will offer whole bean coffee for sale to take home. Some coffee shops even offer multiple roasters to choose from, displayed colorfully on retail shelves. If you need help, ask the barista what they recommend, and try a couple of things on their advice. Buying local has the added benefit of supporting a coffee business in your neighborhood, which is always something we recommend (see page 34).

As with all things these days, the internet offers a broad vista of further options to enjoy. One potential route is to find a compelling subscription service, be it from an individual roaster or a "coffee club" that curates roasters for you, offering a direct portal to interesting stuff for you to try.

Or it might be as simple as picking your favorite city. Maybe you once visited somewhere like Barcelona or London and really enjoyed your time there. Ordering coffee from a roaster in one of these cities will make you feel more connected to that place, even if you can't visit as often as you'd like. More and more coffee roasters around the world ship internationally, and coffee websites such as Sprudge—published by the authors of this very book—offer coffee lovers the opportunity to discover cool roasters and cafes all around the world, from the city you live in to that city you've always wanted to visit.

This is an important thing, actually: coffee bags these days tend to look really cool. There's a good reason for this—beautiful packaging has the ability to inspire purchasing—but we'd like to argue here that packaging design is about more than just commerce. Art in our modern world is increasingly disconnected from everyday life; it costs a small fortune to start an art collection, and these days most people can only interact with art from inside of a museum or an online gallery. But packaging design offers something more immediate, a form of consumable art that looks like a beautiful coffee bag, a stunning bar of chocolate, an eye-catching beer can, or a truly compelling label on a bottle of wine. Today, many talented and interesting artists are working in these mediums, designing consumable art that accompanies the products we love to enjoy and allowing us to enjoy some of their artistry, even if temporarily, in our homes. We think that in the future, people will look back at this era as a truly innovative and important time in the field of consumable art (which is really like a form of popular art if you think about it). Coffee-bag art has a deeper power and resonance than most people give it credit for, and it's one of our very favorite things about coffee today.

On a good day, we might have half a dozen different coffees from roasters around the world in our cabinets. We worked with more than thirty different coffee roasters during the creation of this book, happily brewing, cupping, slurping, and pulling shots from a rainbow of brightly colored coffee bags.

Coffee should be fun—we say this a lot—and coffee bags are undeniably one of the most fun parts of coffee culture today. So shop around, try lots of stuff, and think of this as your own little beautiful art collection. What's inside the bag is beautiful and important, and so is the art you hold in your hands.

"Having lots of different coffees at home—the variety of
it all—speaks to why I love coffee in the first place.
It's like art to me, really. These are just berries,
and they make so many flavors . . . and I find that so
fascinating! It reminds me of when you used to have to
buy a CD to hear music, remember that? You would open it
up, read the credits, pull out the foldout, and absorb
knowledge about who wrote what, who performed on which
track . . . and for me, having lots of coffee bags around
is kind of like that. Where did y'all source this? Okay,
what season? I'm out here reading these coffee bags like
liner notes, and I love it."

**—Propaganda, Los Angeles, California, hip-hop
recording artist and coffee connoisseur
extraordinaire**

You Should Visit Great Cafes

This book is all about making awesome coffee at home, so this
section might feel a little counterintuitive on the face of it. But please hear
us out. An integral part of any considered home coffee practice involves the
regular patronage of fine coffee shops. This is something we feel incredibly
strongly about, so allow us to go a bit deeper.

Coffee shops are the central nervous system of the coffee industry, hubs
of coffee culture, purveyors of a vast collection of collected knowledge
and practices about the art and science of coffee brewing, and important
neighborhood third places in our increasingly disconnected world. They're
also a lot of fun, often boasting gorgeous interior design and top-of-the-line
brewing equipment, from high-end espresso machines and grinders to the
latest and greatest in brewing methods. All of this can inspire your dream
coffee setup at home, and cafes are also great places to get insight on
whatever brewing hiccup you might be working through. They sell fresh and

lovely coffee beans, bagged for your convenience, ready to take home and put through the paces in your latest brewing passion project. Certain cafes even allow you to purchase or take home complimentary water that has been prepared for coffee brewing (see page 14).

These two nodes of coffee appreciation work symbiotically: going to cafes all the time will improve your coffee making at home, and making coffee at home will help you appreciate the hard work of great cafes.

To prove the theory, we'll end this chapter with a brief anecdote from one of the best home coffee brewers we've ever met. His name is Larry Berger, and he's a longtime friend of our website, one of our earliest regular readers and supporters. Larry lives in San Francisco, and his apartment in the Mission Dolores district is home to a world-class home espresso setup, with gear by La Marzocco and Mahlkönig comparable to what you find in a truly great cafe. One afternoon we joined him in his apartment for a couple of coffee drinks and watched as he pulled a half dozen or so espresso shots, dialing in and doing his best to perfect the service before serving them to us. Larry's shots were exemplary and delicious, and we told him so. "That's great," Larry said in response, nonplussed. "Want to walk over to the cafe down the street and see how they're pulling it today?"

In this moment, Larry Berger offered us a really beautiful example of the importance of cafes for the home coffee lover. It's one thing to pull a great shot of espresso at home, and this is an accomplishment no one should take lightly. But the true test is understanding how that shot measures up to how the pros are doing it at the cafe level. There's something refreshingly humble and reverent about this approach, and it's something we encourage you to adopt as part of your home coffee-making practice. You should be darn proud of yourself for making delicious coffee drinks at home; you should also be willing to compare those drinks to what's on offer at your local cafe, because this context represents a challenge and a goal to strive for. There's something meaningful about that.

On a perfect day, we're brewing coffee for ourselves at home, and we're enjoying coffee drinks at our favorite cafes. Sounds like a coffee dream come true.

Part 2

METHODS & RECIPES

Chapter 3

BREW METHODS

Scores of coffee makers have been invented since coffee was
first roasted and brewed. These days, most manual coffee makers fit into three
major categories: pour-over, full-immersion, and forced pressure. From these
three major categories, an endless array of brewers and devices branches off.

For the purpose of this book, we've selected some of our favorites from
these three major categories, but this is by no means an exhaustive list of how
to perfect every last brewing style known to coffee. We welcome you to apply
recipes to other brewers of similar shapes and styles.

Perhaps one of the most pressing questions is how much coffee to use.
This question is tricky for many reasons—manufacturers have different ideas
of what a "cup" measurement is, scoop sizes are inconsistent, and ultimately
it comes down to personal taste. We believe there is a sweet spot for every
brewer paired with every coffee—and the best way to find that sweet spot is
by sticking to a simple brew ratio.

In this book we use a brewing ratio of 16:1 by weight. This means 1 gram
of coffee is needed for every 16 grams of water used. This ratio is a slightly
more coffee-generous ratio than the standard recommendation made by the
Specialty Coffee Association (which is 55 grams per liter, or closer to 18:1).
The use of grams and milliliters is standard practice in the coffee industry
and corresponds to the measurement of weight, as opposed to measuring
by volume with tablespoons or cups. Using weight to measure as opposed to
volume helps with precision and easily corresponds to the use of gram scales
in the home kitchen, which have wonderful further application in other home
kitchen pursuits, such as baking.

Without getting into water chemistry (there are complete and wonderful
books for that), we're assuming that 1 gram of water equals 1 mL. In this book,
milliliters and grams are considered equivalent.

A Note on Scales

Go to any good coffee bar in a city or town near you, and we'll bet dollars to donuts that they'll be using digital scales throughout the brewing process. The digital scale is a wonderful tool to have in the kitchen, and it's particularly conducive to precision and repeatability in the art of coffee brewing. Most of the recipes in this book ask you to use a digital scale not once but twice: first, to measure the whole bean coffee that you'll grind, and next, to measure the water you're brewing with during the brew process itself. This approach is an industry standard and highly recommended. Do yourself a favor and acquire a nice digital scale for your home coffee setup, such as those made by Acaia, Hario, or Escali. A good kitchen shop will be able to help you source one of these, and they are readily available for purchase online.

WEIGHING WHOLE-BEAN COFFEE ON A DIGITAL GRAM SCALE.

CHEMEX BREWING METHOD

Year invented: 1941

Inventor: Dr. Peter Schlumbohm

Country of origin: USA

Grind: Medium-coarse

On our counter: 6-cup

The Chemex coffee maker is an hourglass-shaped pour-over
device that combines both the conical brewing chamber and the carafe. A
filter fits atop the device. Depending on the filter used, it can produce either a
sweet, clean cup or something earthier and more viscous. More on filters later.

Dr. Peter Schlumbohm was an eccentric German-born inventor of countless
patented objects and designs, but the Chemex is his best-remembered
invention. Schlumbohm was inspired by both the Bauhaus school of design
and glass lab gear and also by usability and an intuitive approach, and the
Chemex was his best attempt at an attractive, easy-to-use coffee maker.

Well, mission accomplished. Made of borosilicate glass and traditionally
fitted with a wooden collar and split-grain leather tie, the Chemex was an
immediate hit when it debuted in the 1940s. The Museum of Modern Art hailed
it in 1943 as one of the best-designed home products of the decade, and
today it's been included in MoMA's permanent collection, as well as museum
exhibitions at the Brooklyn Museum and the Corning Museum of Glass.

Certain coffee brewers are timeless, and while the Chemex is not the *only*
icon of coffee-brewing design, it's certainly worth celebrating the brewer's
simplicity, beauty, and cup quality. The Chemex Corporation has put out a
number of products over the years, and now, in the twenty-first century, the
Chemex comes in different sizes and models; for our recipe we're using the
6-cup Classic Chemex—on fine grocery store shelves for around $50.

This 6-cup Classic Chemex can brew as much as—you guessed it!—6 cups
of coffee. Because of restrictions with the brewing vessel itself, practical batch
sizes can be limited—ideally, you have enough coffee ground in such a way
to allow the water enough time to interact and steep with the coffee before
gravity sends it through the filter. Our method uses less coffee and water,
yielding about 20 ounces of delicious coffee. We find this to be the Chemex's
sweet spot, and once you've mastered this recipe, we encourage you to try
bigger and smaller batch sizes, adjusting variables like the coarseness of the
grind and using your sense of taste and smell as a guide.

Chemex coffee can be brewed with third-party paper or metal filters, but
for the full experience, use the triple-bonded Chemex-brand paper filters. The
filters come in two colors: oxygenated (peroxide bleached) white and natural
brown. There are pros and cons to each, but they both do the job just fine.
Both filters are rated as biodegradable and compostable. At Sprudge Labs,
we happily use both bleached and unbleached Chemex filters and encourage
you to experiment with both to determine your favorite.

CHEMEX COFFEE

Makes 20 ounces

640 mL water heated to 205°F (96°C), plus additional for
   rinsing the filter

40 grams whole bean coffee, ground medium-coarse

1 ———— **Place a filter in** Chemex with the three folds against the spout.

2 ———— **Prerinse the filter with** hot water. Pour a good amount of hot
water (about 100 mL) through the filter to both rinse the paper filter
and preheat the Chemex. Allow it to heat for 30 seconds, then
carefully pour the rinse water out, keeping the filter in place and
avoiding contact with the hot water.

3 ———— **Place the ground coffee** in the filter. Make sure that the filter
is sealed to the sides of the Chemex—you don't want any air gaps
that would cause the liquid to bypass the bed of coffee. If the
coffee grounds aren't level, use a spoon or your finger to smooth
out the coffee. Place the Chemex on a scale and tare.

4 ———— **Start a timer and** pour in 80 mL of the hot water—the goal is
to wet all the dry grounds. Gently stir the grounds with a spoon.
The coffee grounds will begin to react with the water and release
gases. (This is called the *bloom*.) Allow the coffee to bloom for
30 seconds.

"I like the Chemex because it's a physical object to have
in my house to really treasure. I like a little bit of
patina on it. A Chemex that's too clean actually makes me
kind of nervous! I use white bleached filters only, and for
me that's partly about getting used to a brewing routine.
Once you get a brewing routine down, you'll feel more
comfortable learning more about origin and regionality.
The whole process unlocks in a beautiful way."

—Matt Rodbard

RECIPE CONTINUES

5 ——— **After 30 seconds, pour** in 150 to 200 mL of the hot water. Keep the pour close to the center unless there are stubborn grounds collecting on the sides of the filter—if so, knock those down with the pour. The goal is to keep the water level just above the coffee grounds. Simply add more water as the coffee brews, always keeping the coffee submerged.

6 ——— **You should finish pouring** what remains of the 650 mL of water at the 3-minute mark. The water will brew through 1 or 2 minutes later. Remove the filter and enjoy your coffee.

BREW TIPS: The Chemex is a snap to clean because the filter pulls out and is compostable. Most days the brewer can be simply brushed and rinsed out after use. For a deeper clean, the handsome wood and leather adornments can be easily disrobed and the Chemex treated with a vinegar and baking soda solution to remove any stubborn coffee residue.

OTHER HELPFUL USES FOR CHEMEX: We love a multipurpose coffee tool, and the Chemex is a veritable Swiss Army knife when it comes to its many uses. Throw a bouquet of flowers in it for a mid-century-modern vase moment. Decant your beautiful bottle of Beaujolais in it during dinner (just rinse it out before dessert). Build a fairy-wonderland terrarium within the Chemex's beautiful bell chamber. Mix up a batch of party drinks and treat it like a punch bowl! Any recipe that steeps, brews, decants, or mixes with an eye toward future pouring enjoyment is a ready friend to the Chemex.

"For me, it's all about making a morning Chemex. A bit paradoxically, now that I have two kids and everything is crazy in the morning, I like brewing my Chemex the most. It takes me about seven minutes to do from start to finish, and that's what I'm focused on. I'm not running around and chasing kids. It's an exciting part of the day for me, it's the morning meditation. Here's my chance to just kind of zone out, not focus on the chaos surrounding me as the children are picking on each other, and after that, you get your first sip of coffee, you get that jolt, and you can return back to your previous state of anarchy."

—Zac Cadwalader, Dallas, Texas, managing editor at Sprudge Media Network

HARIO V60 BREWING METHOD

Year invented: 2004
Inventor: Hario
Country of origin: Japan
Grind: Medium
On our counter: 02 Ceramic

A deceptively simple brew method, the Hario V60 is among a few in this book that demand special attention be paid to the way hot water is introduced to the ground coffee.

A careful, steady stream is almost always essential to a good brew, and our favorite way to achieve this is with a gooseneck kettle. The long spout assists with a gentle shuttling of hot water compared to a more traditional kettle with a wide spout, which pours a little less delicately. We recommend the classic Hario gooseneck kettle paired with this brewing method, which is available in both stovetop and electric options. There are also a number of accoutrements one can buy to resist the flow of hot water from your kettle.

This brewer comes in many sizes, colors, and materials, including glass, metal, plastic, and ceramic. We have the 02 size on our counter—there is also an 01 and an 03, corresponding to small, medium, and large. We prefer the ceramic model, though it requires a preheat before using. Plastic, glass, and copper versions have less heat retention and don't need that additional step. Some people insist on rinsing their filters; others bypass that step—this is ultimately a matter of personal preference.

HARIO V60 COFFEE

Makes 18 ounces

640 mL water heated to 205°F (96°C), plus additional for
   rinsing the filter

40 grams whole bean coffee, ground medium

1 ——— **When your water is** up to temperature, place the V60 filter in the V60. It's helpful to prefold the seam so that when you open the filter, it sits flat against the cone.

2 ——— **Place the cone on** top of a glass server—Hario makes an excellent server that pairs nicely with the V60. Pour a good amount of hot water (about 100 mL) through the filter to both rinse the paper filter and preheat the cone. A ceramic filter takes quite a bit of water to preheat, and if it's not heated properly, that mass will suck the heat out of your brew. Plastic filters, on the other hand, are great insulators and don't need that much preheating.

3 ——— **Place the ground coffee** into the warmed filter. We like making a depression in the bed of the coffee with a spoon or your finger to focus the stream of water and saturate all of the coffee. Place your filter on the scale and tare. Get your timer ready!

4 ——— **Start the timer, then** pour about 80 mL of the hot water on the grounds. Use a spoon or a chopstick to stir up the bed of coffee, being careful not to tear or disrupt the paper filter.

5 ——— **After 30 seconds, pour** what remains of the 650 mL water in a steady stream, initially pouring into the center of the bed, then use the directionality of the stream to evenly distribute the coffee outward in a spiral-motion pour. Be gentle with this pouring motion—you aren't trying to punch a hole in the coffee grounds. Spiraling out of and back in toward the center is a good technique; the objective is to make a circle with your stream of water that's roughly the size of a silver dollar (or Canadian loony), as opposed to pouring straight into the center. A steady stream and this circular motion keep the coffee grounds evenly distributed. Practice makes perfect!

RECIPE CONTINUES

6 ——— **Aim to complete adding** all 650 mL hot water in 2 minutes 30 seconds. Once you are done pouring, gently stir the coffee in the cone again, scraping the sides of the filter. Be gentle, but don't be afraid to give the liquid some direction. The drip-through should finish in about 30 seconds.

BREW TIP: If you decide you don't want to spring for a Hario pour-over kettle, you can make it work with a stovetop kettle. In that case, instead of maintaining a steady stream, try splitting up the main pour (after the initial bloom) into two chunks, and stir a bit in between to make sure all the grinds stay submerged.

"I love making a V60 brew at home using my Baratza Encore grinder to grind fresh beans. I try to stick to a recipe, but it's very hard for me to actually follow the steps and not get distracted, and I think a lot of people can relate to that. Honestly, I just try and enjoy coffee brewing on a V60 as much as I can and not take it so seriously. It's as simple as sticking to a ratio, weighing what I'm using, and then just enjoying it all and having fun with it. I feel that if I take coffee brewing too seriously, it will lose the magic of being a peaceful moment in the morning. That's such an important part of making coffee for myself, because there're no rules, and I need only to please my own palate. It's supposed to be an enjoyable moment."

—Karla Boza, El Salvador, coffee producer, scholar, and expert taster

KALITA WAVE BREWING METHOD

Year invented: 2010
Inventor: Kalita
Country of origin: Japan
Grind: Medium
On our counter: 185 Stainless Steel Wave

The Kalita Wave is a line of capable single-cup pour-over brewers that differentiates itself from brewers like the conical Hario V60 (page 45) and the Zero Dripper (page 65) due to its flat bottom, which creates a flat, even coffee bed for brewing. These brewers use proprietary thin paper filters that are touted to have less paper taste than other filters. The Kalita Wave has been used to win international brewing competitions and is considered by many to be one of the best pour-over brewers in the world. The Wave is available in glass, steel, and ceramic options, with two size variations: the 155 (small) and the 185 (medium). Other flat-bottom dripper options include the December, Gino, Bloom, and Blue Bottle Coffee Dripper. Each of these brewers has their own quirks, but our method is adaptable (with slight tweaks) to any brewer in this style.

KALITA WAVE COFFEE

Makes 20 ounces
640 mL water, heated to 205°F (96°C), plus additional for
   rinsing
40 grams whole bean coffee, ground medium

1 ——— **Place the filter in** the brewer, then pour a good amount (about 100 mL) of the hot water through it to preheat the brewer and rinse the filter. Pour out the water.

2 ——— **Add the coffee to** the filter, set your timer for 30 seconds, then slowly stream 80 mL of the hot water, enough to saturate all the coffee. Give the coffee a stir with a spoon to ensure full saturation.

3 ——— **At 30 seconds, pour** more of the hot water into the center of the coffee bed, and then pour in a spiral outward. Keep the bed saturated and pour in the remaining water slowly enough so that you finish the pour at about 3 minutes 30 seconds.

BREW TIPS: Maintain an even flow rate through the bed of coffee using "pulsed pours." This means adding a bit of water throughout the brew time in literal drips, keeping the water level just above the ground coffee so that it's always barely under a shallow body of water. Aim to slowly introduce 100 mL of the water every 45 seconds.

"I get asked all the time in the education classes I lead, 'How do you brew at home?' My answer is very simple. I truly believe that if you're paying top dollar for a few ounces of single origin coffee, you shouldn't have to experiment with it and waste it to get something that tastes right. I think the Kalita offers a really easy way to get repeatably delicious coffee at home, again and again, and so it's my favorite way to brew. It just tastes good!"

—James Lim, Seattle, Washington, science-loving microbiologist and the founder of Waston's Counter, one of our favorite coffee bars

AEROPRESS BREWING METHOD

Year invented: 2005
Inventor: Alan Adler
Country of origin: USA
Grind: Medium-coarse
On our counter: AeroPress Original

AeroPress is among a handful of brewers in this book invented
relatively recently. Originally it was marketed to make home espresso,
but coffee enthusiasts quickly discovered that this device makes a ripping
filter coffee. In the years since its launch, coffee folks have tinkered with
countless brew recipes—changing variables like water temperature, grind,
agitation, and brew time—and even flipping the whole thing on its head for
an "inverted" recipe (more on this later). Its modest price point and relative
ease of use make this a fun brewer to have in the kitchen, and it's especially
convenient to take with you on the road. The AeroPress brewer is as at home
in your kitchen as it is at a campground or tucked away in your backpacking
kit (the smaller AeroPress Go, released in 2005, is especially great for travel).
The whole world is your coffee bar with the AeroPress. The taste is somewhere
between a filter coffee and a French press. The act of applying pressure
during the brew process sends larger particles through the filter, resulting in
a cup that has more body. Don't be surprised to see some sediment at the
bottom of your mug.

STANDARD AEROPRESS COFFEE

Makes 10 ounces

320 mL water heated to 203°F (93°C), plus additional for
    rinsing

20 grams whole bean coffee, ground to a medium-fine
    consistency (you want a consistency like kosher salt)

1 ——— **Slot the AeroPress paper** filter into the AeroPress basket then screw onto the AeroPress chamber (not to be confused with the AeroPress plunger—that comes later).

2 ——— **Pour a good amount** (about 100 mL) of hot water through the AeroPress to preheat the brewer and rinse the filter. Discard the water.

3 ——— **Place the ground coffee** in the AeroPress, then put the whole thing on your scale and give it a tare (this is important—you'll be brewing directly on top of the scale, measuring your water as you go).

4 ——— **Place your AeroPress on** top of whatever vessel you'd like the brewed coffee to land in: this can be a cup of your choice or perhaps a nice glass coffee server.

5 ——— **Start your timer and** pour a good amount of water, about 200 mL, directly onto the coffee. You might consider rotating the AeroPress along the way to evenly saturate the grounds.

6 ——— **Now give your coffee** a nice stir with a spoon, or use the paddle included with your purchased AeroPress and stir it 10 times. Don't worry if a few drips of coffee make it through the filter at this stage.

7 ——— **Add the final pour** of water, roughly 120 mL.

RECIPE CONTINUES

8 ——— **Take the plunge.** You're waiting for the timer to hit 1 minute 30 seconds, and then you'll plunge for all you're worth, pressing the AeroPress down through the device at a steady pace. This plunge should take just about 30 seconds, making for a 2-minute total brew time.

BREW TIP: The plunger bit of the AeroPress process is worth practicing a few times. Do it dry first so that you get used to creating a seal with the plunger. Soon you'll be plunging with confidence.

INVERTED AEROPRESS COFFEE

Makes 8 ounces

276 mL water, heated to 205°F (96°C), plus additional water
    for rinsing

17 grams whole bean coffee, ground medium-fine

1 —— **Start out doing everything** the same as you did the first go-round: same water temperature, same filter, same rinsing of the filter with hot water, and same grind consistency.

2 —— **Here's where it starts** to get weird. Remove both the AeroPress basket and the filter from the AeroPress, then delicately place the plunger portion of the AeroPress ever so slightly inside the brew chamber, so it sits just inside. This takes some doing—practice this a few times.

3 —— **Start a timer and** add around 175 mL of the hot water to the brew chamber. Stir the coffee as in the first AeroPress recipe (10 times with a spoon or paddle), then add the remaining water.

4 —— **Now it's going to** get truly weird: Make sure the paper filter is slotted in place, then set the filter basket on the AeroPress and make sure the seal is screwed tight. Get a sturdy coffee cup prepared in your free hand. When the timer hits 1 minute 30 seconds, place the mug (held from the handle with faith and hope) upside down directly on top of the AeroPress, grip everything tightly, and flip it all onto a table or counter. Then you can start the plunge. You want to plunge the whole thing down in around 30 seconds.

BREW TIPS: It might seem like tempting fate—this inverted AeroPress business—but coffee types swear that it yields an absolutely delicious cup of coffee and is firmly worth the trouble. One thing to note is that the AeroPress is great at heat retention, and that's why our brewing times for the AeroPress are quicker than, say, a V60 or a French press.

Play, experiment, and generally mess around with your favorite ratios and methods! This little device is surprisingly versatile and has proven itself time and again as a firm favorite.

SIPHON POT BREWING METHOD

Year invented: 1830s
Inventor: Loeff of Berlin
Country of origin: Germany
Grind: Medium
On our counter: Hario TCA-5

The siphon pot, or vac pot, is one of the most theatrical brew methods in our coffee arsenal. It's a thrill to bring it out after a large dinner and delight guests with the drama and the intrigue of vacuum vapors in action.

The method went through a marked vogue around 2010, showing up with increasing regularity at high-end coffee bars and coffee competitions. The method looks sort of intimidating and conveys pageantry and lab-quality authority in nearly any situation. Over the last few years, the method has become less common to find at the cafe level, and we know more than a few people with a siphon pot cluttering up the back of their coffee cabinet, rarely used.

That's a shame. Vac pots can be so much fun, and they're also capable of producing a really beautiful cup of coffee. There are all manners of makers, shapes, and sizes, but the one we've worked with most is the Hario TCA-5. Most siphons come equipped with a spirit lamp as the heat source, but we like using butane torches for their efficiency (and added level of theatrics).

A VERY SPECIAL SPRUDGE NOTE ON SIPHONS: Use caution! Follow the instructions that come with your siphon, and be mindful of the burner and delicate glass! (And see the first Brew Tip on page 59.)

SIPHON POT COFFEE

Makes 17 ounces
560 mL water
35 grams whole bean coffee, ground medium—think sandy
    particles at a tropical beach

1 —————— **Assemble your siphon as** per the factory instructions. Fill the
bottom chamber (or globe) with the water and place this part
of the siphon pot over the burner, then turn the burner up to a
medium-high setting.

2 —————— **While the water is** heating up, prepare your filter by placing it
in the upper chamber of the siphon pot.

3 —————— **Place the top chamber** atop the bottom globe. Once you see
the early makings of a boil (some bubbles forming but not yet
rolling), give it a good twist to seal.

4 —————— **The magic begins!** Water will start rising into the top globe, at
which point you'll want to lower your burner temperature to keep
to a low boil. You're looking for an acceleration in the water rising.
Once you've got that, go ahead and lower the temperature even
further until you can just barely make out the flame. You're shooting
for a brew temp of around 200°F (93°C).

5 —————— **Once the water has** risen into the top chamber, add the coffee
and start a timer. Give the coffee a wee stir, just a few times, to
fully saturate the grounds. Let the mixture sit, and then at about
45 seconds, give the coffee another gentle stir.

6 —————— **At the 2-minute mark,** shut off your burner and pull it out
(gently) from beneath the siphon. You'll see the coffee draw itself
down now, which is fun and beautiful and not always immediate.
Once the drawdown is underway, give the coffee another gentle
stir. Look for a total drawdown time of around 1 minute 30 seconds,
but this is an inexact science (despite how scientific the siphon pot
looks), so don't worry if things go a little quicker or take a bit
longer.

BREW TIPS: There's a lot of drama and excitement involved in the siphon pot process, but please remember to go slow, follow factory directions, and do your level best not to burn yourself or others. Also be mindful of the delicate glass, and avoid putting your hand right through one of the glass chambers, as a co-author of this book once did memorably a decade ago.

It's true that any coffee-brewing recipe should be followed by open-minded taste testing, but when it comes to the siphon pot, this step is especially essential. Taste your finished brew, then go back to the starting point and try again. Adjustments to grind size will have an outsized impact on this particular brewing process, so that's a great aspect of this method to tweak. For example, your "sandy" particles—were they more like Palm Beach sugar or big chunky Mediterranean beach pebbles? This part of the process can always be refined through trial and error.

In a roundabout way, the siphon pot is similar to the AeroPress: extraction time, grind, and temperature are all going to have a pretty distinct impact on the quality of your final brew. It might feel like tempting fate a bit, but we like to err on the side of a higher temperature on our siphon pots, so let that butane crank. The best way to figure out your favorite siphon pot recipe is to just keep practicing and playing with this method, which is honestly quite a lot of geeky fun, like building a coffee version of a kid's Erector set or something. Adjust one variable at a time, play around, have fun, and let your inner science geek freak flag fly.

Between brews, you'll want to be careful about how you store your reusable cloth siphon pot filter. Wash it thoroughly using warm water, allow to dry fully, then place it in a Ziplock bag, and set it away somewhere unobtrusive in your refrigerator awaiting the next brew.

FRENCH PRESS BREWING METHOD

Year invented: 1852

Inventors: Henri-Otto Mayer and Jacques-Victor Delforge

Country of origin: France

Grind: Coarse

On our counter: Bodum Chambord 8-Cup Coffee Maker

This brew method is called many names, and the coffeepot can be made with various materials, including glass, metal, or plastic. Versions of the French press—sometimes called a coffee plunger or cafetière—have been kicking around since at least 1852, when a patent was issued to two French inventors, Henri-Otto Mayer and Jacques-Victor Delforge, for an early version of the brewing equipment. An improved version of the French press was patented again in 1929, this time in the United States by Italian inventors Attilio Calimani and Giulio Moneta. Yet another improved version was patented in 1958 by a Swiss inventor named Faliero Bondanini. Popularized in Europe and the United States during the latter half of the twentieth century, this device has ridden the many waves of coffee and still proves to be a worthwhile candidate for your home coffee setup. Some coffees simply taste better brewed through a French press, and any coffee you really love is worth trying via the method.

It is deceptively simple, making use of a carafe with a fitted lid that contains a metal filter screen. This filter can be deployed by hand using a plunger atop the lid; coffee is allowed to extract fully immersed in hot water for a set amount of time, before the grinds are plunged to the bottom of the container, which is a most dramatic and satisfying motion.

Bodum has been manufacturing sturdy French presses for half a century, and companies like Starbucks and Stumptown Coffee Roasters have sold their brewers for decades. Their Chambord model comes in several makes; we prefer the 8-cup glass carafe, stainless-steel model with a mesh screen filter. We simply adore coffee from the French press and might argue that this full-immersion method offers a true glimpse at the possibilities of coffee as a delicacy.

"The French press was intentionally designed to be used with a coarser grind because it doesn't have a paper filter—it's a mesh filter. But I would suggest that you try to experiment with a medium-size grind. The inventor intended for the French press to be used in a certain way, but for everything we do with coffee, it's important to experiment and have fun with it at the same time. You can appreciate the purpose of coffee and still know that knowledge gives us freedom to use things in all these different ways."

—Daniel Brown, Atlanta, Georgia, owner of Gilly Brew Bar, home to some of the most original coffee elixirs in the world

FRENCH PRESS COFFEE

Note: This is for an 8-cup French press. If you use a smaller or larger French press, consult the manufacturer's instructions for brew ratios. A standard ratio of 15 mL of water to 1 gram of coffee can be scaled up with ease.

Makes 26 ounces

800 mL water, heated to 205°F (96°C), plus additional water
    for preheating

53 grams whole bean coffee, ground coarse (Note: A coarser
    grind helps promote extraction in the French press method.)

1 —— **Preheat French press carafe** and screen with hot water. Empty the rinse water and shake the screen dry over the sink (or place it on a kitchen towel).

2 —— **Place the ground coffee** in the preheated French press, and start a timer as you introduce just enough of the hot water to saturate and wet all the ground coffee. Assist this with a gentle stir using a spoon or chopstick.

3 —— **After 30 seconds, add** the remaining hot water until the slurry reaches the top of the brewing chamber. If you're using a scale, measure 800 mL hot water.

4 —— **Carefully set the French** press lid on top of the brewer without plunging. After 4 minutes have passed, press down the plunger.

5 —— **Let sit for 1 minute**—this allows large particles to sink down to the bottom and results in a cleaner cup. Then serve!

BREW TIP: This recipe has been serving us well for decades, though there's a lot of room for experimentation. Folks report good results with longer extraction times. Instead of 4 minutes, try 5 or 6 minutes, then compare the results! A coarse grind is recommended, but we welcome attempting a finer grind for a different flavor experience. A word of caution: The finer the grind, the harder it will be to press. Too much effort can result in breakage—and an unfortunate mess on your countertop.

MELITTA BREWING METHOD

Year invented: 1908
Inventor: Melitta Bentz
Country of origin: Germany
Grind: Medium-fine
On our counter: 1-cup

Melitta has become a sort of household name for coffee lovers,
and chances are you're already familiar with Melitta's iconic line of coffee
filters, which are sold in grocery stores around the world. (They're the ones in
the green and red box.) What you might not know is the charming backstory
of how Melitta came to be a force in the coffee lives of millions.

It all starts in '08—that's 1908, thanks—when inventor Amalie Auguste
Melitta Bentz was struck by an unusual bolt of inspiration. A piece of blotting
paper from her son's schoolbook inspired her to use that same paper to filter
out excess coffee grounds. She experimented with household items to perfect
the method, and in 1908 she was awarded a patent by the Imperial Patent
Office in Berlin for "coffee filter with rounded and recessed bottom perforated
by slanting flow-through holes using filter paper"—one of the very first coffee-
brewing equipment patents of the modern era.

More than one hundred years later, the Melitta brand remains strong,
trusted by coffee professionals and casual coffee drinkers alike in homes and
cafes all over the planet. For this recipe, we focus on both the Melitta filter
and the Melitta brand 1-cup brewing cone, although the cone is available in
several cup sizes. The Melitta cone offers a distinct version of the pour-over
style of coffee brewing, but much of our standard approach to these brewers
can be adapted to the Melitta.

MELITTA COFFEE

Makes 10 ounces

320 mL of water heated to 205°F (96°C), plus additional for
    rinsing

20 grams whole bean coffee, ground medium-fine (you are going
    for the consistency of beach sand)

1 —————— **Place a filter in** the Melitta cone with the filter crease folded.
(folding the filter at the seam helps it sit properly in the brewer).

2 —————— **Prerinse the filter with** hot water to preheat the Melitta.
Carefully pour the rinse water out, keeping the filter in place and
avoiding contact with the hot water.

3 —————— **Place the ground coffee** in the filter. If the coffee grounds
aren't level, use a spoon or your finger to smooth out the coffee.
Place the Melitta on a scale and tare.

4 —————— **Start a timer and** add 64 mL of the water—the goal is to wet all
the dry grounds. Gently stir with a spoon. The coffee grounds will
begin to react with the water and release gases, or bloom. Allow
the coffee to bloom for 30 seconds.

5 —————— **After your timer reaches** 30 seconds, begin to pour 150 to
200 mL of the hot water into the brew. Keep the pour close to the
center, unless there are stubborn grounds collecting on the sides of
the filter—knock those down with the pour. The goal is to keep the
water level just above the coffee grounds, adding more water as
the coffee brews and always keeping the coffee submerged.

6 —————— **You should finish the** full 320 mL pour at the 1 minute
30 second mark, and the water will brew all the way through
shortly. Remove the filter and enjoy.

BREW TIP: A gooseneck kettle will give you increased control of your water,
especially when it comes to step 5—it's easier to chase those stubborn side
grounds down into the filter with a focused spout of water. If you're skipping the
gooseneck business entirely, we advise you to pour slowly and maintain extra
attention throughout.

ZERO DRIPPER BREWING METHOD

Year invented: Late twentieth century
Inventor: Zero Coffee
Country of origin: Japan
Grind: Medium-fine
Sizes: Small, large
On our counter: Small

The Zero Dripper, or Bee House as it was once branded in the
United States, represents an update of sorts, or perhaps a refinement, on the original cone-shaped pour-over filter invented by Melitta in 1908 (see page 63). Over the years, the Zero has earned an ardent fan base, and to a casual coffee drinker, it might be hard to tell the finished cups apart. What exactly is the difference between the Zero and any other cone-shaped brewer?

We think the answer goes beyond mere style, although the Zero is indeed a stylish brewing apparatus. It all comes down to flow rate: the shape of the Zero's cone is sloped *just so*, and the brewer's row of drip holes helps promote fluid thermodynamics conducive to stable, reproducible brewing parameters.

You can be forgiven if your eyes glaze over, and it's not our goal to get really technical as to why one brew method is better than another. All you need to know is the Zero is a beautiful brewer that makes great coffee in a style similar to the Melitta but slightly differently in a pleasing way. It's a great addition to any home-brewing arsenal.

ZERO DRIPPER COFFEE

Makes 10 ounces

320 mL water heated to 205°F (96°C), plus additional for
    rinsing

20 grams whole bean coffee, ground medium-fine (think beach
    sand)

1 ——— **Place the filter in** the cone with the filter crease folded.

2 ——— **Prerinse the filter with** hot water to preheat the cone, and carefully pour the rinse water out.

3 ——— **Place the ground coffee** in the filter. If the coffee grounds aren't level, use a spoon or your finger to smooth out the coffee. Place the cone on a scale and tare.

4 ——— **Start a timer and** introduce 64 mL of the water—the goal is to wet all the dry grounds. Gently stir with a spoon, and allow the coffee to bloom for 30 seconds.

5 ——— **Pour 150 to 200 mL** of the hot water into the brew, incorporating any of the stubborn grinds that may have collected halfway up the paper. You might swirl your pour or work in figure-eight shapes, but be sure to pour consistently and keep as much of the coffee submerged as possible.

6 ——— **You should finish your** 320 mL pour at the 1 minute 30 seconds mark, and the water will brew all the way through shortly. Remove the filter and enjoy.

BREW TIP: There's a good chance that your favorite local coffee roaster—or one of the several nice roasters you've ordered coffee from—are currently offering a delicious washed arabica coffee from a Central American nation such as El Salvador, Honduras, Panama, or Guatemala. There is a wide world of variation within this category—different coffee varieties, different approaches to coffee washing, and of course different roasting methods—but as a general rule, washed coffees from Latin America just absolutely sing when brewed through a Zero Dripper. It is a great place to start your brewing adventures with this particular method.

CLEVER DRIPPER BREWING METHOD

Year invented: Early twenty-first century
Inventor: Absolutely Best Idea Development (ABID) Company
Country of origin: Japan
Grind: Medium-fine
Sizes: 300 mL and 500 mL
On our counter: 500 mL

The Clever is a full-immersion brewer with a familiar pour-over shape. The secret is the locking mechanism that keeps the brew water and coffee in constant contact until a spout is released upon placing the device on a mug or carafe. In this way, the Clever sort of splits the difference between a pour-over cone and a full-immersion brewer like a French press, resulting in the potential for creating a cup that offers the best of both worlds.

In terms of popularity, the Clever has never quite had the name-brand cachet of Chemex, nor does it boast the in-every-home ubiquity of the French press or Melitta. It is not a design icon like the moka pot, and it's not a culturally tangible representation of coffee expression like the phin or the espresso machine. All it does is brew a pretty damn fine cup of coffee—and for that, the Clever is more than enough.

CLEVER DRIPPER COFFEE

Makes 10 ounces

320 mL water heated to 205°F (96°C), plus additional for
    rinsing

20 grams whole bean coffee, ground medium-fine (you want
    grinds that are slightly dialed back from the fineness
    of a French press)

1 ——— **Place the filter in** the Clever with the filter crease folded.

2 ——— **Rinse the filter with** hot water to preheat the Clever. Carefully pour the rinse water out.

3 ——— **Place the coffee in** the filter. If the coffee grounds aren't level, use a spoon or your finger to smooth out the coffee. Place the Clever on a scale and tare.

4 ——— **Start a timer and** introduce 64 mL of the water—the goal is to wet all the dry grounds. Gently stir with a spoon and watch the coffee bloom.

5 ——— **After your timer reaches** 30 seconds, begin to pour the rest of the hot water into the brew. You should finish your 320 mL pour at the 1 minute 30 seconds mark, and the water will brew all the way through shortly. Remove the filter and enjoy.

BREW TIP: The Clever Dripper has an odd, cultlike fan base: "Once You Go Clever, You Go Back Never" is their rallying cry. While we'd never choose to settle down with just one brew method, it is undeniable that the Clever Dripper is remarkably well-adapted to getting nuance and flavor out of just about any coffee. A delicate washed coffee from Latin America, a floral and bright heirloom Ethiopian, a natural processed coffee from Indonesia—all of these are going to be beautiful in the Clever. You kind of can't go wrong, honestly, and the more you start using this brewer, the more you'll find yourself reaching for it again and again.

NEL DRIP BREWING METHOD

Year invented: 1800s to 1920s

Country of origin: Japan

Grind: Coarse

Sizes: Varied

On our counter: 240 mL Hario Nel Drip

The Nel Drip is also sometimes known as a woodneck or a coffee sock, and it's easy to see why: it more or less looks like you're brewing coffee through a little sock! We actually really love this method, although it's not too common in US cafes, and it's more likely something you'd see at a specialty coffee bar in Japan. There is also a long-standing and proud tradition in Costa Rica that uses a similar brew method known as the *chorreador*, so if you get the chance to travel to Costa Rica for coffee, you'll definitely see it there.

This method utilizes a wild brew ratio, a cloth brewer, and a significantly lower brewing temperature. The lower temperature yields a different flavor profile, which some feel is sweeter and richer. The amount of coffee used is rather shocking for the minimal amount of water used, so pay attention to brew ratios in this recipe.

As proselytizing coffee lovers, we low-key want to inspire a renewed appreciation for the Nel Drip. Put it like this: if we show up at your coffee shop and you're offering a Nel Drip, we are going to order it, take photos of the whole thing, and compliment you on your derring-do and appreciation for obscure brewing methods. And the same thing absolutely goes for brewing at home. Let's rock with the sock.

NEL DRIP COFFEE

Makes 3.5 ounces

185 mL water heated to 175°F (79°C), plus additional water
    for rinsing

45 grams whole bean coffee, ground coarse

1 ———— **Pour hot water through** your clean, dry brewing "sock." (We do not literally mean like a tube sock. We mean the cloth provided with your purchase of a Nel Drip brewer.) Discard the rinse water.

2 ———— **Add the ground coffee** to the sock filter. It looks like a little bundle of joy!

3 ———— **Over 45 seconds, slowly** add 45 mL of the hot brew water, saturating the dry ground coffee.

4 ———— **Pause for 45 seconds** to allow the coffee to become fully saturated.

5 ———— **Add 80 mL of the** hot water in the center of the brew bed, circling outward, for about 60 seconds. Allow the water level to decrease for 20 seconds.

6 ———— **Add the remaining 60 mL** hot water over a 30-second period of time. Allow water to draw down and transfer to preheated mug. The total brew time should be about 3 minutes 30 seconds.

BREW TIP: All of our advice with other methods applies here: practice makes perfect, feel empowered to tweak your recipes, try lots of different coffees, and so forth. But to this general advice we want to add one more thing . . . take lots of pictures! The Nel Drip is kind of adorable looking at every step of the process, and documenting your brewing adventures visually is part of the fun.

PHIN DRIPPER BREWING METHOD

Year invented: 1850s
Country of origin: Vietnam
Grind: Coarse
Sizes: Varied
On our counter: 6-ounce dripper

We just adore the phin brewer and think it's really underrated among fancy coffee types.

The small cup-shaped phin has a filter chamber and a lid that allows coffee to be slowly brewed. Entering your cup via a drop-by-drop drip, phin brewing creates a nicely concentrated coffee. Each drop provides an opportunity to slow down, take time, relax, and savor the process. Much like a V60 (see page 45) or AeroPress (see page 52), the phin filter utilizes a unique way of brewing coffee that is also very convenient and earth-friendly. It's often made from stainless steel or aluminum, it doesn't require paper filters, and it comes in a number of sizes, ranging from 4 ounces all the way up to 12 ounces. The phin also provides a beginner-friendly brewing method that is effective and easy for anyone to understand.

For many, the phin brewer is synonymous with traditional coffee styles in Vietnam, a country with a huge story to tell when it comes to coffee appreciation, coffee growing, and absolutely delicious local coffee culinary practices. Our first exposure to the phin came from eating at great Vietnamese restaurants around the Pacific Northwest, where we grew up. These places were often using pre-ground coffee with robusta in the blend, either roasted and imported from Vietnam or via roasters in the United States (Café du Monde of New Orleans is one popular option). In recent years, Vietnamese coffee traditions have received meaningful recognition and reappraisal by a new generation of entrepreneurs, so you're increasingly seeing the phin dripper utilized with practices that are more common in contemporary coffee brewing, such as fresh ground coffee beans and relatively lighter roast profiles.

PHIN DRIPPER COFFEE

Makes 2.5 ounces

15 grams whole bean
coffee, ground very
fine (think fine table
salt; go for really
small particles on
this one)

100 mL water, heated to
200°F (93°C)

1 ——— **Place the filter plate** on top of the mug or carafe, then place the brew chamber on top of the filter plate. Add finely ground coffee to the brew chamber. Make sure the coffee bed is even so that when you top the grounds with the gravity press, it's nice and level. Place on the scale and tare.

2 ——— **Pour 30 mL of the** hot water over the gravity plate. Allow coffee to bloom for 30 seconds before adding more water.

3 ——— **Add the rest of** the water and allow full immersion. It will take about 2 minutes before the first drips come out of the brewer, and the entire brew will finish in 5 minutes' time.

BREW TIPS: The resulting coffee will be viscous and thick. One popular way to enjoy this brewing method is as a cà phê sữa dá, in which the phin brewer sits atop a glass filled with ice and sweetened condensed milk. The dripper brews directly over the milk and ice, creating a delicious, creamy, sweet iced coffee drink that's ready to enjoy on a hot day.

As with any filter, be sure to clean your phin thoroughly after using, making sure there aren't any coffee particles sticking to the drip holes.

MOKA POT BREWING METHOD

Year invented: 1933
Inventors: Luigi di Ponti and Alfonso Bialetti
Country of origin: Italy
Grind: Fine to medium-fine
Sizes: 1-cup, 3-cup, 6-cup, 9-cup, 12-cup
On our counter: 6-cup

We can't help but smile when we think about the moka pot,
another icon of early twentieth-century coffee design, this time by way of
Italy. For a nation so closely associated with espresso, the moka pot offers a
glimpse into how many Italians still choose to brew coffee at home.

And about that coffee. This method is one of forced pressure as opposed
to pour-over or full-immersion. This results in a totally different cup profile, one
that some find reminiscent of Americano-style espresso, and others don't care
for much at all. It's true that your finest, most nuanced bag of rare, expensive
Gesha coffee might not be the first choice for the moka pot—the method itself
is going to blunt some of the more nuanced, floral characteristics of a coffee
type like that, which is better suited for brewing with your best pour-over
method. But we don't make the rules, so feel free to do whatever you want
with your moka pot. It's worth cherishing any excuse to get things percolating.

MOKA POT COFFEE

Makes 11 ounces
20 grams whole bean coffee, finely ground
345 mL of water heated to 205°F (96°C)

1 —————— **Prep your filter by** filling the funnel with the ground coffee to the top. Don't press or tamp down on the coffee.

2 —————— **Fill the lower chamber** of the moka pot with the almost-boiling water to the fill line or valve.

3 —————— **Carefully screw the top** on (the lower chamber is hot—we use a towel), and place the moka pot on the stovetop. Turn the stovetop on to medium heat.

4 —————— **Coffee will begin to** brew—look for a nice, even flow of coffee as it brews. If it's choking or halting mid-brew, your coffee may be too finely ground. Once the lower chamber nears empty, you'll hear a sputtering. Remove the moka pot from the heat, and place the lower chamber under cold water to stop the brew process completely.

5 —————— **Enjoy a piping hot** cuppa moka pot.

BREW TIPS: It's essential that you use hot water from the start, which will reduce the overall brew time of the moka pot and help avoid over-steeping. This is the same principle as preheating a cast-iron pan to sear a steak—in our experience, there are fewer bitter flavors and less astringency when starting with hot, near boiling water.

Consider pairing a moka pot brew with a nice whip of frothed milk using our home French press milk frothing technique (see page 118) for a low-tech homemade cafe au lait.

The rough-and-ready moka pot makes a handy inclusion to your camping kit and can even be brewed over the campfire! Just make sure you bring along gloves that can handle the heat when it's time to pour and serve.

COLD BREW BREWING METHOD

Around these parts, we call it "chilly sauce"—but by any name, there's no denying the fact that cold brew's growing popularity is widespread, and in the early twenty-first century, this brewing method has become an important aspect of the business of coffee.

In all probability, your first experience drinking cold brew probably happened at a coffee shop or from a ready-to-drink can or bottle of cold brew from a retail store. There are some absolutely delicious ready-to-drink cold brew options on the market today: our favorites are from brands like Stumptown Coffee, Blue Bottle Coffee, and Riff. Chances are your local cafe also offers its own take on cold brew, which is well worth exploring.

But cold brew is also easy and inexpensive to make at home. Some roasters like Stumptown even encourage this by offering a "Cold Brew Blend," coffees that are roasted together with cold brew in mind as the brewing method. Using a basic technique—and a little patience—you can make delicious cold brew at home with ease.

This recipe makes a cold brew concentrate, and the finished product can be cut with equal parts water or milk—or not! It won't kill you to drink it straight up.

Cold Brew Tips from a Pro

Brent Wolczynski helps run things over at Stumptown Coffee's cold brew division. We asked him to give us a little input on cold brew; there's nobody we know who does more work with this stuff day in and day out. "Generally a 5:1 weight ratio is right on for making a cold brew concentrate," says Brent. "And I definitely recommend room temperature water for your jar while the coffee is extracting. Don't put it in the fridge; colder water slows down the extraction and can result in a cold brew that tastes sour."

Rinsing the so-called sparge is an important step that Brent likens to a similar technique in beer brewing in which grains are rinsed at the end of the brewing process to extract as much usable product from them before filtering. "Rinsing is important for making cold brew, because it helps increase extraction efficiency for the finished product and makes the most use of your coffee grounds.

"To me, there are different ways to make coffee and they're all good," says Brent, who recommends chocolatey, sweet Latin American washed coffees for cold brewing at home. "Cold brew is just a different expression of what coffee can be. Cold brew to me feels quenching and simple, with a pleasant sweetness and acidity. It's what I want on a really hot day."

COLD BREW

Makes 20 ounces

120 grams whole bean coffee, ground medium-coarse

700 mL filtered room-temperature water for brewing

Special Equipment:

1 clean mason jar (Note: Consider running it through your
    dishwasher before using, or sterilize it using hot water
    direct from your kettle.)
Cheesecloth
1 large colander
1 large bowl, sterilized in the same way as the jar
1 paper filter

1 —————— **Place the mason jar** on your scale, then put the ground coffee in the mason jar. Add 600 mL of the filtered room-temperature water. Give the water and coffee a good stir to get it nice and saturated, then cover the jar with cheesecloth, secure with a rubber band or string, and place it somewhere dark and out of the way—a kitchen cabinet is great or toward the back of your counter space. Let the mixture sit for at least 14 hours—doing this overnight is a sensible choice.

2 —————— **After your long, fortuitous** wait (or the next day), line the inside of the colander with more cheesecloth, and place it over the sterilized glass bowl. Dump the mason jar full of cold brew into the prepared colander, grinds and all, and let the brew strain through the cheesecloth.

3 —————— **Rinse the cold brew** grounds (or "sparge," a loan term from beer brewing) with the remaining 100 mL of filtered room-temperature water. Allow the water to work its way through the sparge and into the bowl below.

4 —————— **Now that you've got** a bowl full of cold brew, it's a good idea to filter it once more using a paper filter. Strain the cold brew through a paper filter into your preferred storage vessel—perhaps a

RECIPE CONTINUES

nice bottle or another clean mason jar. This cold brew concentrate is now ready for your consumption enjoyment and could be mixed in a ratio of 1:1 with filtered water, mineral water, soy milk, or another beverage of your choosing (dark rum works like a charm). Store cold brew concentrate for up to 1 week in your refrigerator.

BREW TIP: Some cold brew methods don't include an extra filtering step, but we think it's essential for the quality of your brew. When it comes time to filter, Melitta, Technivorm, and Hario all make paper filters that are perfect for chilly sauce—avoid using a Chemex filter as they can be a bit too dense for your delicate brew.

Brewing to Our Favorite Songs

Throughout this book, you'll find us calling out various brew times, sometimes down to the second. That's because timing is a really important part of brewing coffee—and paying attention to timing is essential in producing a delicious brew—no different than baking a cake or ending a meeting.

But with forgiveness and grace toward this bedrock fact, isn't there something rather . . . soulless about all this timer business? Setting a timer on your phone and following that timer to the letter is good for getting started, but once your home coffee routine becomes more self-expressive and begins resembling something like a personal ritual, we think it's okay to think outside of the timer app box.

Music is another field where timing is critical, and the length of a given song is one of the most common pieces of information in how music is conveyed—in many cases, it's easier to learn how long a song takes to listen to rather than who actually wrote it. The world of music is actually a world of timing, and by fusing music and coffee together, we're able to craft a new sort of intentionality around the passing of time.

Music can make coffee taste better, and coffee can make music sound better. Here's a few suggested songs to brew to, paired with some of the methods covered in this book, but—as is hopefully quite obvious by now—this is personal, and you should already be thinking up your own favorite music pairings to brew and sip alongside.

AeroPress
2:30-minute brew time
Ann Peebles, "I Can't Stand the Rain" (2:30)

V60
2:30-minute brew time
Slum Village, "I Don't Know" (2:35)

Nel Drip
2:30-minute brew time
Crosby, Stills, Nash & Young, "Our House" (2:59)

Zero Dripper
2:45-minute brew time
Perfect Mother, "Dark Disco-Da-Da-Da-Da-Run" (3:08)

Kalita Wave
3:30-minute brew time
Fiona Apple, "Every Single Night" (3:30)

Clever Dripper
4:30-minute brew time
Klaus Nomi, "The Cold Song" (4:20)

Automatic Machine
5-minute average brew
XTC "Garden of Earthly Delights" (5:02)

French Press
5-minute brew time
The Roches, "Hammond Song" (5:46)

Chemex
7-minute total production time, from grind to pour
Sylvester, featuring Patrick Cowley, "Do You Wanna Funk?" (6:54)

Siphon Pot Brewer
7-minute production time
NYC Peech Boys, "Don't Make Me Wait" (7:14)

Coffee Ice Cubes
Roughly a 3-hour freezing time
Magnetic Field 69, *Love Songs* (the complete three-disc album) (170 minutes)

Cold Brew
A 14-hour total process
The Grateful Dead, *Dick's Pick* vol. 1–12, featuring live concert selections from 1970 to 1990. A long, strange trip (840 minutes)

"I strongly believe that coffee correlates with music on so many different levels. One demands taste and another demands sound, but they both have notes. And something artistic inside of me makes me connect with them together in a deeper way."

—Daniel Brown

Chapter 4

THE CHALLENGING, REWARDING WORLD OF HOME ESPRESSO

Over the years, we've come to realize that our jobs—coffee writers—mark us as fairly unusual beings to the kind folks we meet on airplanes, in taxicabs, or across the occasional cheeky bartop. There aren't a lot of coffee writers, much less full-time coffee writers who have been at it for a decade. And so when someone finds out this is what we do for a living, inevitably there is a follow-up question or set of questions seeking opinion from us on a caffeinated matter close to this dear stranger's heart. Across the last decade, some of the questions have changed (we used to get asked a lot about "cat poop coffee," but not so much anymore), but one has remained fairly constant and of great urgency to the general public: What home espresso machine do you recommend?

Well! We're all for recommendations—this book is full of them—but the answer to this question is more like a psychological survey, a Rorschach test, and a Zen koan rolled into one. The right home espresso machine is no mere A or B matter; to answer this question properly, we have to talk about what espresso machines really are, what they're built to do, and why you want one in your home in the first place. From there we can do our best to divine what might be the correct choice for you to make, should you still choose to make it after listening to our spiel.

The quest for cafe-quality espresso at home is like the coffee world's version of the hunt for Bigfoot: many have searched, and some have claimed success, but the evidence of proof is flimsy at best. The truth is espresso is a mode of coffee brewing predicated on high volume: the best environment for espresso making is in a busy cafe with dialed-in professional equipment operating at regulated temperatures staffed by professional baristas. It's very difficult to reproduce this experience at home and can be an expensive boondoggle, leading to kitchen cupboards cluttered with dusty cast-off devices of dubious repute.

It doesn't have to be this way. In years past, we may have told you to simply save your money and walk to your nearest quality coffee shop for an espresso. But it's time for a reappraisal of this advice, as advancements in home espresso technology and knowledge have helped usher in a new era of opportunity for crafting delicious espresso drinks at home. Making espresso at home takes time, money, trial and error, and dedication. It's more than just a habit, it's a hobby; but for those who pursue it, there is no sweeter reward.

This is a long way of saying, we have a take—kind of a lengthy take, in fact! Please settle in as we now give it to you as fulsomely and informatively as we know how.

"Honestly, making home espresso is like learning anything else, any other difficult skill. You have to be willing to do it wrong a bunch of times. And along the way you may mess around and find out that something 'wrong' is actually what you like! It is what it is. Feel authorized to experiment and get stuff wrong. Don't be precious about it.

"But there're some basics you need to follow. You gotta clean the portafilter between each shot, and you need to use good water. Upkeep is important, especially if you're using a high-quality espresso machine. It costs too much not to take care of it.

"You might want to buy a less expensive machine to start, or even a manual espresso machine, or something like the AeroPress (see page 52) as a first step. For me that's like, well—there's nothing like performing live on a bad karaoke mic in a dive bar full of drunk people who don't care and trying to hold their attention. Nothing will teach you how to be onstage better than that, rather than trying to jump into rocking an arena or a YouTube studio. Play on a crappy stage to understand how your voice works. I think it's the same when you're pulling shots. Go mess up, go work on a cheaper machine, so that you learn what you need to learn the hard way."

—Propaganda

GRINDING COFFEE INTO A PORTAFILTER ON A LA MARZOCCO MAZZER LUX D ESPRESSO GRINDER.

Is Home Espresso Right for You?

Once upon a time (like, in our first book), our blanket answer to the home espresso question was simply "Don't bother—just go to a cafe." There's a reason for this, aside from us being lifelong cafe obsessives who think about espresso bars the way other people think about fine-dining restaurants. Making espresso at home is finicky. It requires several sorts of investment: time, money, care, space, and skill, to name just a few. But the availability of excellent home espresso machines has grown considerably in the last five years, and the pandemic only served to draw more attention to making quality coffee drinks at home. And so today, when we talk about home espresso machines to friends and strangers, we start by asking a question: "Is home espresso right for you?"

Turns out it's a deceptively complex question, the sort that begets *more* questions, like a Talmudic exercise or riddle of the Sphinx. But we're asking because we want you to avoid a common occurrence in the home coffee-making world, in which the thing you spent hundreds of dollars on now languishes in the back of your cupboard or in a box in the basement. This should never be your fate.

When you envision a home espresso experience, what are you thinking about? Is it cafe-quality coffee drinks involving meticulously prepared shots of espresso and frothy, steamy milk? Are you producing these drinks yourself, on demand, each morning with a minimal investment of time? Are you making drinks on this machine once a day or several times a day, or will your home espresso machine occasionally double for use in a light commercial setting, like at a coffee pop-up or particularly rambunctious dinner party? Is espresso primarily your focus, or are you an all-latte, all-the-time sort of person? How about a mocha, a steamer, a matcha creamer? Are you going to make five drinks a week, or fifty, or five hundred?

And why do you *really* want a home espresso machine? Is it for convenience? Do you consider it a cultural investment? Are you tired of going out to a coffee shop? Is there no good coffee shop within twenty miles of your home? Do you kind of resent how much money you're spending at the coffee shop, and so you're thinking about a home espresso machine primarily as a cost-benefit-analysis sort of thing, built more from frugality than obsession?

The truth is, for most people—not all, but most—investing in a home espresso machine doesn't make a ton of sense. If you're thinking about home espresso as a casual thing, or a way to "save money," or the sort of party trick you plan on pulling out only twice a year at big group dinners, we honestly don't think home espresso is the right call. A great many of you reading this chapter will be better served by semiregular visits to your quality-focused local coffee bar of choice, where top-of-the-line equipment, attention to detail, and machine maintenance are part of what you pay for in that $5 latte. (It's a bargain, all things considered.) Otherwise you are going to wind up with another box in your basement.

But for some of you, the idea of having a home espresso machine is a passion, a hobby, the sort of thing you could see yourself getting really into, like fixing up a motorcycle or mastering the potter's wheel. You plan on cleaning your espresso machine regularly, caring for it, showing it off to friends and family, delighting the coffee lovers in your inner circle and, most importantly, pleasing yourself. Deep down, your dream kitchen has *always* been home to an espresso machine, and you consider the whole thing to be a form of functional art, gourmet and gastronomic and invigorating.

"So you want to do espresso at home? Well, why? Do you enjoy the craft? Do you think it's fun? Or do you just want to have a great espresso from time to time? If that's all you're looking for, you should really just go to the best local cafe in your area when you want to drink espresso drinks.

"But if you enjoy the routine of making espresso and find that routine to be cathartic, well . . . I say go for it. But you need to ask yourself: What am I really trying to get out of this practice? And how much am I willing to spend? Questions grow other questions when it comes to espresso at home, but I do know one thing for sure. There's a huge underplaying of how hard it is to be a barista. A bartender gets tipped a dollar for opening a bottle of beer; a barista gets tipped that same dollar for conquering the endless variables required to make dialed-in espresso shots taste delicious. And there's nothing like getting into making espresso at home to bring this all into perspective."

—James Lim

For those of you of this mindset—the true heads—home espresso is a wonderful habit, a fulfilling hobby, and a lifelong pursuit. To these readers, we recommend the following espresso machines.

The Quest for the Perfect Shot

INTRODUCTORY EQUIPMENT (SUB-$1,000)

Honestly, we nearly considered leaving this section blank or else writing a pithy "Don't bother" or something similarly glib. But the truth is the road to good intentions is paved with underperforming home espresso machines that cost less than $1,000. And if you do end up buying one, you should think of it as a stepping stone, the proverbial "starter home" of espresso machines, something to prove your interest in the hobby—but not, in all likelihood, the final destination in your home espresso journey.

If you simply must purchase that which is recognizably an espresso machine, and you must do it at this sub-$1,000 price point, the Breville Barista Pro and Rancilio Silvia are the best in this limited category. Both are single-boiler machines with a small footprint made by a reputable manufacturer, and both are capable of steaming milk, though it's nothing like what you'll get at a good cafe. The Breville machine uses an integrated conical burr grinder and an LCD touchscreen. The Rancilio is decidedly more analog, and you'll need to pair it with a grinder. Both companies offer more upscale versions of home espresso grinders, but their entry-level offerings are sub-$1,000, and Breville's also includes an innovative home coffee subscription, which is a fun way to try lots of different roasters.

BREWING ESPRESSO OUT OF A PORTAFILTER ON A LA MARZOCCO LINEA MINI ESPRESSO MACHINE.

Better purposed for this price category are several very good home espresso grinders—you'll need a good grinder, after all, if you intend to pursue the hobby of making espresso at home. Most of the top brands in the world of grinders are making a home-worthy grinder in this price range, including the Mahlkönig X54, the La Marzocco Lux D by Mazzer, and the Baratza Sette.

> "I think the most important thing for coffee brewing is the right grinder. The grinder is like the knife for a chef—if you don't have a really good knife, you can't produce beautiful food; you'll never be able to cut your tomato with precision and technique. It's the same with a coffee grinder. Having a quality grinder helps the coffee taste better."
>
> **—Freda Yuan**

INTERMEDIATE OPTIONS ($1,000 TO $5,000)

With more budget to spare, the possibilities for creating a quality home espresso experience begin to reveal themselves. Let's not take this amount of money lightly; $5,000 is a lot to spend on anything. But if you're going to get seriously into the practice of making quality espresso at home, this is part of the investment, along with time, care, maintenance, and education. (Nobody said it would be easy.)

The aforementioned Rancilio and Breville both have worthwhile offerings in this range, including the Breville Oracle (which has a built-in grinder as well as two boilers) with easy-to-use touchscreen display and subscription coffee access, and the Rancilio Silvia Pro X, which also sports a dual boiler and impressive temperature stability. Elsewhere in the price range, the Profitec Pro 800 lever machine gives you hand-pulled, retro espresso satisfaction, and it's a beautifully handsome machine to design a kitchen around. There are also ardent fans of products from brands like La Pavoni, Lucca, and Rocket. In late 2022, La Marzocco of Florence introduced a sub-$5,000 espresso machine for the first time. Dubbed the La Marzocco Linea Micra, it retails at about $3,900 and is a smaller version of the La Marzocco Linea Mini, about which you'll read more in the next section.

Under the rubric of a $5,000 budget, you can quite simply purchase the finest home coffee grinders in the world, including the Mazzer Mini Doserless, Baratza Forté BG, and the aforementioned line of products by Mahlkönig, whose grinders have an ardent fan base in the world of fancy coffee.

GO BIG OR GO HOME ($5,000 AND UP)

As we have established, the art and science of enjoying espresso at home requires commitment. Money is not the *only* important part, but there are some things in life where the more expensive option actually is markedly better. There is a significant step up in functionality, effectiveness, and performance available as you go up the pricing ladder in the home espresso machine category; moreover, if your goal is to replicate the drink qualities possible at a busy, calibrated coffee bar, you're going to need equipment that rises to a cafe standard. Otherwise, you really are better off simply going to a cafe.

Our advice for grinders from the previous sections holds—look to a Mazzer, a Mahlkönig, or a Baratza, and feel free to consider things like space and aesthetics. This is your dream home espresso setup, after all.

But on the topic of *the* home espresso machine, well—for perhaps the only portion of this book, we're going to be avowedly mono-brand. There is one clear top-of-the-line product option; it starts at around $5,600 and with bells and whistles can easily rise from there. It's made by La Marzocco of Florence as part of their La Marzocco Home line, which includes custom sales support, continuing education, and maintenance. The machine is called the La Marzocco Linea Mini, a shrunk-down version of the Italian brand's iconic Linea espresso machine—once the espresso machine of choice for Starbucks and still regarded by many as the premier commercial espresso machine in the world today.

The Linea Mini features dual boilers, thermal stability, temperature control, connected app capabilities, and an internal pump system to rival many commercial machines. Indeed, you might well consider it to be a "light commercial" home machine—the Linea Mini powers many a coffee cart and food-truck coffee bar worldwide. From the group cover to the machine's body to the steam wand's wood and its dials, every inch of the Linea Mini is customizable—you'll notice a particularly handsome unit anchoring many of the espresso drinks featured in this book.

When the Linea Mini debuted in late 2014, it represented a sea change in the possibilities and capabilities of espresso at home, and today it's really the only home espresso machine we avowedly recommend without caveat or hesitation. Yes, it's expensive, but sometimes in life you get what you pay for, and chances are if you're *really* serious about this whole home espresso thing, you'll end up buying one anyway after starting with a more entry-level machine. Paired with a Mazzer Lux grinder, you've got cafe-level espresso-making capabilities tooled for the home setting. The next part is up to you: to learn the drinks, the craft, and the tradition of espresso making, and from there to make it your own, to express yourself with these tools, combining a hundred years of espresso-making technology, art, and inspiration into something uniquely your own.

LA MARZOCCO LINEA MINI ESPRESSO MACHINE.

ESPRESSO SHOT

The espresso shot was introduced in 1901 in Italy. Espresso serves as the base ingredient for most cafe beverages. Your favorite mocha, latte, cappuccino, macchiato? You'd better believe there's espresso in it. But espresso, on its own, is a remarkable drink. At its best, it's like shining a microscope on a specific coffee, magnifying the unique flavors and properties in a pleasing and balanced cup.

Italians have adopted espresso into their cultural identity as the go-to breakfast drink of choice. Quick, easy, and served in a demitasse. Boom boom. Elsewhere in the world, espresso often serves as more of a complement to milkier beverages. Find the right cafe though, and a shot of espresso could be a life-changing experience. You'll sometimes also see espresso referred to by the number of shots in the cup: solo (single), doppio (double shot), or quad (four shots, Zachary's favorite).

The process of making a shot of espresso is as simple as following these easy steps and also as complex as your newest lifelong hobby. This is deceptive marketing; the drink is simple and also endlessly difficult to perfect, a fusion of machine and human touch, hard to master and so very rewarding. You should think about pulling a great shot of espresso at home like trimming a bonsai tree or fixing a dusty old car or raising a child. You won't get everything right all the time. The point is that it's something you have to work on every day—but if you really love that work, you will in the end be proud of the results. Espresso is hard, espresso is easy. It's a lot like life. There is no end point, only the journey.

Makes 1 shot

1 —— **Rinse and clean your** portafilter basket, then wipe it with a clean towel so it's completely dry.

2 —— **Dose your coffee from** the grinder. Some espresso grinders (see page 91) will auto-dose for you to an exact amount. Recipes vary wildly, but start with 16 grams and go from there.

3 ——— **Distribute the ground coffee** evenly across the top of the portafilter using a distributor tool, a helpful little metal device that evenly levels out the coffee grounds. If you don't have one of those, simply use your finger.

4 ——— **Tamp down your coffee.** Proper tamping takes practice, consistency, and experience. Talk to experts, watch videos, and chat up your local barista for tips.

5 ——— **Put your portafilter into** the espresso machine, and brew right away. Use a timer to pay attention to how long your shot takes. When you hit 1.5 ounces (or 3 tablespoons) of volume in the demitasse, finish the shot.

6 ——— **Shuck the puck into** your knockbox—the purpose-built garbage container for holding spent coffee grounds—then wipe the portafilter clean and dry before brewing the next shot.

BREW TIPS: Allow us to reiterate here that espresso preparation is infamously difficult to perfect with consistency. Whole books—entire careers!—have been built around this fact. Here is where referring back to some of the earlier conceptual suggestions in this book becomes so very important, namely that coffee brewing should be fun, and everybody should lighten up and relax about it. The only real rule is that there are no rules, just some tried-and-true suggestions to get you where you want to go.

If your shot is too sour, perhaps your espresso is too fine, and you should try adjusting the grind to be slightly coarser. Conversely, if your espresso is astringent, you might tighten the grind into finer particles.

There's no need to rush enjoying your shot! Allowing a shot of espresso to cool slightly (for no longer than 5 minutes, say) is often recommended by smart baristas, and there's nothing wrong with stirring before enjoying.

AMERICANO

An Americano is simply a blend of espresso and water. Espresso, a concentrated brew, is diluted with water and either served hot or iced. When served hot, the cup used is similar to that of filter coffee.

Americanos come in all strengths and sizes. A typical 12-ounce Americano will have a double shot of espresso and 8 to 10 ounces (275 mL) of near-boiling hot water. We recommend adding the espresso to the top of the hot water, essentially "floating" it, which better maintains the crema's integrity.

Modify this beverage by adding flavors, adjusting temperature, and adjusting espresso amount. The most traditional espresso-to-water ratio is a simple 1 to 4: 1 part espresso to 4 parts water. This can be expanded higher or lower depending on the preference of the drinker. One particularly popular derivation looks more like 1 part espresso to 1½ parts water in what's known colloquially as a Little Buddy or an Italiano (this drink has many different names around the world). Another riff uses 4 shots of espresso over ice in a 16-ounce glass, which is then filled to the top with cold water for an Iced Quad Americano—repeated consumption of such a drink was essential to the production of this very book. Though steamed milk is not part of this drink's creation, the Americano, once completed, is a wonderful canvas for a nice splash of your favorite cream or alternative milk.

Makes 1 Americano
Water heated to 180°F (82°C), volume to taste (see headnote)
    or ice cubes (for 1 Iced Americano)
1 espresso shot (1.5 ounces, or 3 tablespoons, roughly
    equivalent to a double shot)

FOR HOT AMERICANO

1 ——— **Start by adding hot** water to a mug.

2 ——— **Pull shot of espresso** into a demitasse or shot glass.

3 ——— **Pour the shot of** espresso into your mug or glass.

FOR ICED AMERICANO

1 ——— **Place a little bit** of cold water in a glass.

2 ——— **Pour in the espresso** and top with ice.

3 ——— **Add more cold water** to taste.

CAFFE LATTE

The caffe latte, or in some places, latte for short,* is an espresso beverage made with steamed milk and topped with milk foam. Specialty cafes will top these drinks with art made by manipulating the espresso and textured milk.

Caffe lattes are served in an array of sizes, though most commonly 8, 12, 16, and 20 ounces. Pay attention to your cafe's menu, and look for the amount of espresso they put in their beverages—typically, a 12-ounce latte has a double shot of espresso. Going a size up might not indicate more caffeine; it could just mean more milk. Ask your barista for clarification.

You can make a caffe latte at home using espresso or concentrated filter coffee. You can create textured milk foam at home using devices like a milk frothing wand, or even a French press (see page 118), or the steam wand on your home espresso machine. Try not to scald the milk, as this may affect the delicious flavor of the creamy steamed milk.

Makes 8 ounces
1 espresso shot (1.5 ounces, or 3 tablespoons, roughly
    equivalent to a double shot)
Milk of your choice, to taste (whole milk is the classic choice,
    but if you prefer soy, almond, or oat milk, go for it)

1 —— **Pull your espresso into** a shot glass or directly into a cup or mug.

2 —— **Using a milk steamer,** frothing wand, or a French press, steam the milk to 140°F to 160°F (60°C to 71°C). For an extra hot latte, you can steam until 180°F (82°C).

3 —— **Pour the freshly steamed** milk into the cup or mug containing the espresso.

4 —— **Serve immediately.**

---

* Note that ordering simply a *latte* in Italy will yield a glass of milk.

CAFFE MOCHA

The caffe mocha is an espresso-based beverage with chocolate and steamed milk. Think of mochas like a hot chocolate with a kick! They are often served with whipped cream on top, though they sometimes also come topped with a bit of milk foam and latte-style foam art, featuring a dramatic contrast thanks to the chocolate. This drink can even be served with a dusting of cocoa powder, depending on the whims of the barista and what's popular in different regions of the world.

For such a seemingly simple drink—espresso, milk, chocolate— the mocha has a surprising and beguiling history. Unlike, say, the cappuccino or the Americano, whose true creators are unknown, the mocha might even have a proven point of origin—the very first cafe where the practice was popularized and invented. That would be Caffè Al Bicerin, in Turin, Italy, where a drink called the *bavaresia* made from (you guessed it) chocolate, coffee, and cream was popular in the early twentieth century. Over time this drink became known as the Bicerin in honor of the cafe and also as a tribute to the small glass in which the drink was served. Back at this time, the drink was made in a sort of choose-your-own-adventure way, or what a chef at a fancy restaurant might called "deconstructed," meaning that you had to actually mix the chocolate in yourself at the table.

At some point they started doing it themselves behind the bar at Caffè Al Bicerin, and the modern mocha was born. It grew in popularity across Europe and eventually landed in America as the "mocha latte," which most people just call a mocha these days (or maybe a "mochaccino," which is fun to say). But where did the name come from? We don't actually know. The first place to use this term—like the true inventor of the Flat White—is lost to history. But it's quite clear that the name "mocha" borrows its existence from the famed port of Mokha, in Yemen, long one of the most important coffee ports in the world. Some even think that since Mokha was known for shipping out naturally processed, sun-dried coffees from Yemen with a chocolate-forward flavor profile that the drink was named in honor of the coffee it most resembled.

That sounds like an old coffee tale to us, but it's a fun one, nonetheless. Like coffee, chocolate has a long history of global trading, colonial distribution, and a modern renaissance for quality and equity in the supply chain. The chocolate you choose for your mocha is every bit as important as the coffee.

Makes 8 ounces

0.5 ounce (1 tablespoon) chocolate syrup, plus more (optional) for serving

1 espresso shot (1.5 ounces or 3 tablespoons, roughly equivalent to a double shot)

6 ounces (¾ cup) milk of your choice

Cocoa powder (optional)

Whipped cream (optional)

1 —— **Place the chocolate syrup** in the bottom of a mug or cup.

2 —— **Pull a shot of** espresso into a shot glass or directly into your mug.

3 —— **Using a milk steamer,** frothing wand, or a French press (see page 118), steam milk to 140°F to 160°F (60°C to 71°C).

4 —— **Stir the espresso and** chocolate vigorously, then pour in the freshly steamed milk.

5 —— **If desired, top with** cocoa powder, whipped cream, more chocolate sauce, or some heavenly combination of all three. Serve immediately.

CAFFE MACCHIATO

The caffe macchiato can be confusing—there's probably no coffee drink in the modern world more responsible for consternation, with the possible exception of the Flat White. Allow us to explain.

The traditional caffe macchiato has been around for as long as folks have had steamed milk and espresso. At its core, this drink is a shot of espresso "marked" (*macchiato* in Italian) with a small dollop of foam, which is served directly in the espresso demitasse. Over time there's been a bit of riffing and innovation from clever baristas, who might use a spoon to scoop and place the milk foam (as is tradition in Italy), but who might also free pour milk from the steaming pitcher directly into the demitasse. Some even top a macchiato with latte art, resulting in a drink that's both small and beautiful and feels more like drinking a mini-latte.

Both of these styles—the poured steamed milk or the dollop of foam— result in a petite beverage where espresso dominates, but milk is allowed to flavor and texture the coffee. It is a delightful drink, something certain espresso blends and single-origin coffees are perfectly suited for, and has long been one of our firm favorite drinks both at the cafe and at home.

But the macchiato does not end there. In 1996, Starbucks Coffee Company introduced a drink they called the Caramel Macchiato, which has gone on to become a signature beverage for the company. This drink is *not* small but instead is served hot or iced in sizes from 8 to 24 ounces and contains espresso, vanilla syrup, milk, and a butter caramel topping.

If you go into a third-wave cafe and order a macchiato, do not expect a Starbucks-style beverage, dripping with ooey gooey caramel. Conversely, if you order a macchiato at Starbucks and you're looking for the traditional version, as opposed to the caramel riff, make sure to specify with your barista.

At home we like making classic macchiatos! Here's our tried-and-true recipe.

Makes 3 ounces
1 espresso shot (1.5 ounces, or 3 tablespoons, roughly
    equivalent to a double shot)
1.5 ounces (3 tablespoons) milk of your choice

1 ——— **Pull the espresso shot** into a demitasse.

2 ——— **Using a milk steamer,** frothing wand, or a French press, steam
the milk to 140°F to 160°F (60°C to 71°C).

3 ——— **Spoon the foam atop** the espresso or free pour a layer of
steamed milk into the demitasse. Either way is valid and delicious,
and you should feel free to experiment to your personal taste
and preference.

CAPPUCCINO

The macchiato and the cafe latte all have their fans, but there's nothing quite like a properly executed and luxuriously enjoyed cappuccino. For starters, what a name! It derives from the Capuchin order of Italian friars; the color of espresso mixed with milk froth is said to evoke their brown and cream robes. Like so many of the terms we use for coffee today, it is a loan word from Italian, but every coffee lover in the world knows it by heart (even if we sometimes forget that third "c").

Today's modern cappuccino is a wonderful beverage and can vary significantly in style depending on where you are in the world, resulting in a vast range of expressions and creations all under the banner of cappuccino. While there are exceptions, cappuccino is usually served hot. It's not uncommon for cappuccino to be served with a dusting of cinnamon or cocoa; this is particularly popular in Australia and New Zealand and, indeed, may have contributed to the name Flat White, used today around the world to describe a short, undusted latte.

Follow the recipes on the next page and foam away.

ITALIAN CAPPUCCINO

Makes 6 to 8 ounces

1 espresso shot (1.5 ounces,
   or 3 tablespoons, roughly
   equivalent to a double shot)
2.5 ounces milk (whole milk
   strongly preferred)
2.5 ounces milk foam

Traditional Italian cappuccino calls for one-third espresso, one-third steamed milk, and one-third milk foam.

AMERICAN QUAD CAPPUCCINO

Makes 20 ounces

2 espresso shots (3 ounces, or
   ⅜ cup, or roughly equivalent
   to 2 double shots)
8.5 ounces milk (if you want to
   be really American about it,
   insist on oat)
8.5 ounces milk foam

You might be saying, "Dang, that's a big cappuccino"—well, everything is bigger in America. This is an extra-large cappuccino, built on a double shot of espresso, in a style commonly ordered in American coffee bars.

BONE-DRY CAPPUCCINO

Makes 8 ounces

1 espresso shot (1.5 ounces,
   or 3 tablespoons, roughly
   equivalent to a double shot)
6.5 ounces milk foam

The bone-dry cappuccino variation uses milk foam that has been stretched to a soap suds–like texture. The foam is then scooped into the vessel atop espresso. The cup's weight is mostly from the espresso and very light.

EXTRA-WET CAPPUCCINO

Makes 8 ounces

1 espresso shot (1.5 ounces,
   or 3 tablespoons, roughly
   equivalent to a double shot)
6 ounces steamed milk
0.5 ounce milk foam

The extra-wet cappuccino variation, opposite, uses steamed milk and very little milk foam. It is, essentially, a caffe latte.

CAFFE CON PANNA

When we first started getting into coffee, the con panna was a coffee-shop standard, and it served as a kind of gateway drink for us to appreciate espresso drinks. We might not have been cool enough in our teens to sip espresso straight, but something about the comforting layer of sweet whipped cream in the con panna helps it all make sense.

Now in the comparatively mirthless days of adulthood, there's nothing that gives us a jolt of joy quite like a good caffe con panna. The whipped cream covering a demitasse is a thing of beauty, and sipping a decadent shot of espresso through a layer of the cool creamy topping makes for the most marvelous hot 'n' cold contrast.

If it's been a few years since your last con panna, you're in for a treat, and the drink couldn't be easier to make.

Makes 3 ounces

1 espresso shot (1.5 ounces, or 3 tablespoons, roughly
equivalent to a double shot)

1.5 ounces (3 tablespoons) of fresh whipped cream (a healthy
dollop will do it)

1 —— **Pull a delicious shot** of espresso into your favorite demitasse. (If you've got something on hand that's roasted a touch darker, this is a great use for it.)

2 —— **Add a healthy dollop** of whipped cream on top of said demitasse. You want enough whipped cream to fully cover the cup, but not so much that it overflows or becomes architecturally unstable.

NOTE: Take your time with your con panna! Sip the espresso through the cream—maybe dunk a demi-spoon into the shot and pull up some cream, then repeat the process. We love these served as part of a multicourse dinner, after the entrée but before the proper dessert.

AFFOGATO

There might not be much we collectively agree on as a society, and at times it feels like consensus is impossible to find. But this we do know: everyone, and we mean *everyone*, enjoys a nice affogato from time to time.

This is perhaps the simplest and most delicious of any cafe drink, and that's why you're likely to see the affogato show up on restaurant dessert menus. They're easy to make at home as well, which is lovely for our purposes.

Somewhere in all this cultural colliding—quality espresso, delicious ice cream—the modern affogato has gone pretty far beyond the typical vanilla-or-chocolate binary. Some of the most interesting flavor combinations come about quite unexpectedly, like one recent affogato we tried that featured honeydew melon ice cream with a shot of natural Ethiopian coffee. Delicious!

Here's a dead-simple recipe for the affogato, plus a few flavor combinations we've tried and loved.

Makes 5.5 ounces
1 espresso shot (1.5 ounces, or 3 tablespoons, roughly
    equivalent to a double shot)
4 ounces (½ cup) ice cream of your choice (see page 110)

1 ——— **Pull a shot of** espresso into a shot glass.

2 ——— **Place the ice cream** in a dish and pour the espresso over it.

RECIPE CONTINUES

Recommended flavor combinations:

- Jeni's Butter Cake Ice Cream with Intelligentsia Black Cat Espresso
- McConnell's Sweet Cream with Go Get Em Tiger Minor Monuments
- Milk Bar Cereal Milk ice cream with Joe Coffee NYC's The Daily
- Rocky Road with Puff Coffee Spirit Lifter
- Pistachio ice cream with espresso of choice (trust us)
- Cold brew float with Tillamook Old-Fashioned Vanilla—a classic flavor combination for a reason.

"There is no coffee treat more delicious, and more forgiving, than the affogato."

—Kyle Glanville

Chapter 5

COFFEE IN THE KITCHEN

The joy of coffee at home does not start and stop with brewing.
Coffee is a marvelous culinary substance, capable of intertwining with and
enhancing a broad spectrum of dishes. Coffee has been a popular flavor
in desserts for hundreds of years, reaching back to the cafe society era of
Vienna starting in the late 1600s. Other applications are more modern and
can be indulged throughout a good meal, from steak rubs to gravy and
custard, as well as sodas, shrubs, and fermented drinks.

The bag of coffee you hold in your hands is many things—including
a wonder of international trade, artisan coffee growing, and meticulous
roasting—but above all else, it is an ingredient that should be played with in
the kitchen with joy and abandon. Let's embrace coffee's culinary possibilities.
We absolutely love cooking with coffee—in the pages that follow, we'll share
a few of our favorite recipes.

PERFECT COFFEE SYRUP

The creation of a delicious coffee syrup is one of the simplest and most delicious ways to employ a bag of coffee. Making this yummy syrup is easy, and the ways to use the resulting product are literally endless—we are still coming up with ideas. For the coffee, feel free to use a quick-and-easy batch brew, or brew using a paper filter in a pour-over method such as Chemex (page 41) or Zero Dripper (page 65). You are looking for a filtered brew with very little sediment.

Makes 180 mL (¾ cup)
250 mL (1 cup) brewed coffee
250 grams (1 cup) white sugar

1 —— **Combine the brewed coffee** and sugar in a heavy-bottomed saucepan on medium-high heat.

2 —— **Bring the mixture to** a boil, then reduce the heat to low and simmer for 10 minutes, stirring occasionally. You'll notice the color start to darken, and the mixture will have reduced by one-third.

3 —— **Decant the hot mixture** into a heat-proof container (with a lid) and allow to cool.

4 —— **Once cooled, seal the** container and place it in the refrigerator. The coffee syrup will keep for up to 1 month, although we promise you that you'll use it all before this time frame elapses.

Here are some of the inexhaustive ways we enjoy our homemade coffee syrup:

> **Over SHAVED ICE.** We put this in all caps because we feel quite strongly about this. Coffee syrup over a fluffy bed of shaved ice is one of the finest coffee treats known to man. Home countertop shave ice contraptions are readily available on the internet and can be found for sale in select grocery

stores. Or if someone in your community makes rad shaved ice, consider teaming up with them and sharing your delicious homemade coffee syrup in the spirit of collaboration. This sweet treat—perhaps served with an additional squirt of shaved ice or alongside flavors like sweet melon or nectarine—is the very culinary pinnacle of hot weather relief.

Add to ice cream. It's great with vanilla, but that's just the start—flavors like sweet cream, malt chocolate, cherry, and pistachio can all be happily topped with tasty coffee syrup.

Toss in an all-day cook. Anything from a dash to a glug of your coffee syrup will add depth and complexity to your trusted recipe for chili con carne, braised beef, or all-day Sunday red sauce. Some recipes, like one for a really gorgeous red mole sauce, might already call for coffee. Feel free to sub in our syrup—just use discretion when considering amounts. We also love this flavor paired with good gochujang sauce, such as in a tteokboki, a braised rice-cake dish with cabbage—use just half a shot of the coffee syrup here.

Red-eye gravy time. We respect the red-eye gravy tradition, though it's typically the sort of food we'd trust to a good diner. If you have your own favorite approach to making REG, invite your coffee syrup to the party.

Coffee egg cream. Spice up your favorite egg cream recipe with equal parts chocolate and coffee syrup. (Make sure you use Fox's U-Bet for the chocolate.)

Allow us to impart some confidence to you regarding your coffee syrup: this stuff is like the philosopher's stone of cooking with coffee at home and can be applied across both savory and sweet dishes. In a braise, it offers a layer of quantum complexity, deepening earthy flavors and drawing out brighter tones. But it's also absolutely incredible popped into your favorite recipe for zucchini bread, carrot cake, chocolate chip cookies, or fruit-and-cream trifle. Batch up our recipe—1 part sugar to 1 part brewed coffee—and make larger amounts of syrup in one go. A little bit here, a little bit there, almost like you might use red wine or vanilla extract, allowing its complexity to layer and accentuate flavor across a broad spectrum of dishes.

WEST VILLAGE SPECIAL

New York City is a special place to us. It's the city we've visited more than anywhere else: Zachary lived and worked at some really great cafes there for a few years, and Jordan might have crashed on a Brooklyn couch or two one long hot summer in the late aughts. And in the pantheon of iconic New York City coffee drinks, we are drawn inexorably toward the utterly incredible coffee soda known as Manhattan Special. Cold, sweet coffee ambrosia! Dark and impossibly smooth! The Manhattan Special is an "espresso soda," with a recipe dating back to 1895. The drink itself is thick and sweet, but there's so much going on in terms of the complexity in the soda's deep, dark flavors.

We can't always get Manhattan Special out on the West Coast, and so we've undertaken an earnest effort to make a reverent version of the drink at home. We start with our basic Perfect Coffee Syrup recipe (see page 114) and tweak it for this particular soda build, which intentionally employs darker flavors (sometimes called "strong" or "robust") in the creation of an earthy, sweet coffee elixir. We recommend making this drink with mineral water as opposed to, say, club soda, because a higher TDS mineral water results in a beautiful creamy mouthfeel of cream and vanilla flavors. The goal in this drink is for the sweet, dark-roasted coffee syrup to shine through, and the creamy mineral touch is a perfect complement. And we've renamed it the "West Village Special" because that's where you'll find us in NYC—we'll meet you at Julius', one of America's most important historic gay bars.

Makes 1 drink

45 mL (⅛ cup) Perfect Coffee Syrup (page 114), made using dark-roasted coffee such as Starbucks French Roast, Intelligentsia El Diablo, or BLK & Bold's Dark Roast Blend, rested in the refrigerator for at least 48 hours

90 mL (⅓ cup) sparkling mineral water, preferably Gerolsteiner (see Note)

1 medium ice cube

1 ——— **Using a Boston shaker** or a glass pitcher, combine 1 part dark-roasted coffee syrup to 2 parts mineral water. Add 1 medium ice cube and stir 13 times clockwise to incorporate.

2 ——— **Place in the refrigerator** to rest for 5 minutes.

3 ——— **If you, by chance,** own a bottling line, this is a great time to bottle your very own homemade West Village Special. If you do not have a bottling line, consider serving your West Village Special straight up in a cafe water glass, or stash it away in a glass flask or small mason jar.

A NOTE ON MINERAL WATERS: Gerolsteiner is a readily available mineral water from Germany, and it works beautifully in our West Village Special. But feel authorized to experiment with other mineral waters of the world, such as Borjomi (Republic of Georgia), Tŷ Nant (Wales), or Saratoga (New York State).

A NOTE ON SERVING: A classic Manhattan Special comes in a distinctive bottle, ready to drink straight from the long neck. You could serve yours on the rocks—it would be especially nice with pebble ice—or drink it straight up. And if a splash of Fernet or Punt y Mes finds its way into your glass, well, we won't tell.

FROTHING MILK
IN A FRENCH PRESS

Steamed milk on demand is undeniably one of the great benefits of having an espresso machine at home. In this book we talk about why home espresso machines are increasingly a great choice for interested coffee lovers and also why the art and science of brewing great espresso drinks at home is no casual affair. It takes time, attention to detail, practice, humility, and maybe even a little bit of gumption in order to brew espresso at home in a way that's comparable to what you might get at a great cafe. And, even then, the odds are stacked against you.

But what about steamed milk? Well—if you want truly *steamed* milk, you need an espresso machine to do it right. But if that's not an option for you or not something you're interested in, there is another method available that actually produces some pretty awesome milk foam to use in a wide variety of coffee drinks.

We are referring to the French press.

Yes, the French press, typically associated with the brewing of full-immersion coffee (see page 60), can also be happily retconned into the on-demand milk frother of your dreams. A Bodum brand French press works great here, but whatever brand you have on hand should do the trick.

We, too, were dubious until we embarked on the process of writing this book. It took some trial and error, and we also drew upon our decade of experience as coffee journalists covering high-level coffee-brewing competitions around the world. (It's a thing.) Turns out that milk foam can be achieved via the use of a French press. Here's our method to try at home—if you do it right, you can even pour latte art with this stuff, which is a trip! Believe us now, and after your jaw picks up from off the floor, try for yourself. All this is possible with the right technique.

SPRUDGE FRENCH PRESS FROTHY MILK METHOD

Milk of your choice
   (choose the amount
   based on your desired
   coffee drink)

1 —————— **Start with a clean** French press and a milk pitcher. Warm the milk to 140°F to 160°F (60°C to 71°C) on the stovetop or in the microwave. (Yes, a microwave, it's fine.)

2 —————— **Transfer the warmed milk** to the French press pot.

3 —————— **With the plunger attached,** start pumping the milk through the mesh filter. Pump vigorously! Pump as though your life depends on it! The milk will quickly double in volume and develop undeniably foamy characteristics.

4 —————— **Give the milk a** good swirl in the French press to fold in foam that may have separated.

5 —————— **Once the milk has** doubled in volume and become fully incorporated, transfer it to a milk pitcher if you'd like to attempt latte art—or simply pour the milk into your coffee drink.

BREW TIP: Invite a small group of coffee lovers over to your home to enjoy a Nice Coffee Time. After a few brews of filter coffee and perhaps an espresso shot or three, abscond to the kitchen so as to prepare a few milk drinks. Follow our French press method for milk foam, but *do not tell your friends.* Return with beautiful milky drinks, presented with lovely latte art. Wait until someone finally asks: "Wait, I didn't hear an espresso machine—how did you make this latte art?" Then inform them that you've followed the Sprudge French Press Frothy Milk Method as depicted in this incredible coffee book. Your friends will be impressed and inspired enough to purchase a copy for themselves.

HOT SPRUDGE SUNDAE

We believe coffee should be enjoyed in a myriad of ways—a beautiful filter coffee and an exquisite espresso shot are both incredible means to experience the complexity and unique qualities of coffee itself. But why stop there? Why not enjoy all the meats of our coffee stew?

Presenting the Hot Sprudge Sundae: a mashup between a classic diner hot fudge sundae and an elevated espresso affogato (page 109). While "Sprudge" isn't actually a portmanteau of *espresso* and *fudge*, the two ingredients are a classic flavor combo. Top with a maraschino cherry and crushed nuts. It's heaven in a sundae bowl and a snap to whip up.

Makes 1 sundae

1.5 ounces (3 tablespoons) hot fudge sauce

1 shot espresso (1.5 ounces, or 3 tablespoons, roughly
    equivalent to 1 double shot)

½ cup McConnell's Sweet Cream Ice Cream (or vanilla ice cream
    of your choice)

A healthy dollop of whipped cream, for serving

Maraschino cherry and crushed nuts, for garnish (optional)

1 —— **Place a sundae bowl** in the freezer to chill.

2 —— **Using a double boiler,** warm up the hot fudge just enough to allow it to pour freely—it should be about the consistency of molasses.

3 —— **Transfer the warmed fudge** to a small bowl and pour in the espresso. Stir until combined. Allow the mixture to cool for 1 to 2 minutes.

4 —— **Scoop the ice cream** into the pre-chilled sundae bowl, then gently pour the hot Sprudge mixture over the top. Top with whipped cream, garnish with nuts and a cherry (if desired), and serve immediately.

BREW TIP: Espresso is the preferred brewing method for this recipe, but specialty instant coffee works well (see page 16). Cut the water by three-fourths to create a concentrated brew.

SPRUDGE MOCHA MADNESS MILKSHAKE

Milkshakes are *so* delicious. They're also a great way to combine some of the collected recipes in this book into a delicious package. For our special choco-licious rendition on a coffee milkshake, we're starting with a base of coffee ice cream, adding a splash of our homemade coffee cold brew, sweetening things up a notch with our homemade coffee syrup, and creating a vision of mocha fantasia by adding a dose of chocolate. Ground coffee beans add visual interest and a pleasing crunch, but they're totally optional.

Makes 1 milkshake

2 scoops coffee ice cream (we like Tillamook)

1 squirt chocolate syrup (we like Ghirardelli)

Good splash of cold brew, about 22.5 mL (¼ cup) (see page 78)

1 barspoon (1 teaspoon) Perfect Coffee Syrup (see page 114)

Ground coffee beans (optional—6 or so will suffice)

Whipped cream, for serving

1 ——— **Add the coffee ice** cream, chocolate syrup, cold brew, and coffee syrup into a blender. Blend on low to your desired creaminess, 2 to 3 minutes. (Preferred milkshake texture is a matter of extreme personal preference. If you want a creamier shake, add more ice cream. If you want a more pourable shake, thin the mixture with a bit more cold brew.)

2 ——— **Add the ground coffee** beans, if using, and pulse once more to distribute. Serve in a milkshake vessel of your choosing and top with whipped cream.

COFFEE CUSTARD

What's better than warm, unctuous, eggy custard? It's a staple in so
many of the desserts we love. A simple custard is a beautiful thing,
but we've gussied up ours a bit by including—you guessed it—coffee. We
use specialty instant here—we like Joe Coffee's version, but any good
specialty instant is your friend for this recipe. We're aware that this
ever so slightly deviates from the "what to do with a bag of coffee"
concept expounded at the top of this book, but you know what? Having
some specialty instant around to bake with or to drink in a pinch
(like if you're stuck at sea) is a sound policy. There's a reason why
flavor crystals, coffee extracts, and the like have long been favored by
bakers: they allow you to add a strong coffee flavor to a dish without
significantly impacting a given recipe's liquid volume. This is why
that lab-made "coffee" flavor permeates so many of the coffee things
we enjoy. But you can do better! Try it this way, with some new-wave
specialty instant.

Coffee custard in this style is not unlike a good "egg coffee"
drink that is popular across Southeast Asia—we've enjoyed lovely versions
here stateside at restaurants like Berlu (Portland) and Breadbelly (San
Francisco). The big difference between that and this, as far as we can tell, is
that a dessert custard gets cooked until creamy on the stovetop—long enough
to coat and cling to your whisk—whereas an egg coffee remains a steady
drinking viscosity. Otherwise, they're firmly siblings from the same eggy coffee
galaxy.

Note: Be patient making your custard. It takes time, and if you've never
done it before, you might feel as though the process is a tad laborious.
But if done right, at the end you wind up with a pourable, wobbly coffee
custard that's happily at home in a parfait, in a trifle (with lots of vanilla
cake), topped with fresh whipped cream and berries and enjoyed straight,
or maybe sandwiched between a couple of oatmeal cookies.

Makes 1 50-ounce (1.5-quart) pot of custard (6 to 8 servings,
    depending on how much the person being served loves custard)
500 mL (2 cups) whole milk
500 mL (2 cups) heavy cream or whipping cream
100 grams (½ cup) superfine or caster sugar (we like C&H
    Baker's Sugar)
6 large egg yolks
Half packet (5 grams or 1 teaspoon) specialty instant coffee
    (we recommend The Daily by Joe Coffee)

RECIPE CONTINUES

1 ——— **Pour the milk and** the cream in a medium heavy-bottomed saucepan. Add 50 grams (¼ cup) superfine sugar. Whisk lightly to integrate.

2 ——— **Slowly and carefully bring** the mixture to a simmer over a low heat. You're looking for a few bubbles to appear around the sides of the dish—but not a boil. Go slowly! Do not rush this step; 20 minutes is about right but will vary depending on the saucepan you use. Relax, put on a podcast, there's no hurry.

3 ——— **While the mixture is** coming to a simmer, beat the egg yolks in a heatproof pitcher or pouring bowl with the remaining 50 grams (¼ cup) superfine sugar.

4 ——— **Pour the hot mixture** from the saucepan into the heatproof pitcher. Whisk thoroughly to combine.

5 ——— **Now pour this mixture** back into the saucepan, still over a low heat. Stir constantly with a wooden spoon for about 10 minutes. And be patient—you are looking for a glossy, smooth, soothing consistency to the custard, so that it clings to the back of the wooden spoon yet remains pourable.

6 ——— **At the last moment,** add the instant coffee to the saucepan.

7 ——— **Give a last few** hearty stirs with the wooden spoon, then remove the pan from the heat. Strain the custard through a metal sieve into a heatproof jug pitcher.

8 ——— **You should definitely serve** at least some of this coffee custard immediately so as to appreciate its warm, comforting texture, but it also does nicely in the refrigerator for up to 3 days. If refrigerating, place in a plastic container with lid affixed, or cover the jug with plastic wrap. You can reheat before serving or simply serve cool.

COFFEE BBQ SPICE RUB

Perhaps you've noticed that there is SO MUCH coffee spice rub on the market today. It seems like every city has its own version, and it's something we welcome and celebrate as lovers of all things coffee. But in our own homes, we've developed an approach to the coffee spice rub that leans into using that fresh bag of coffee currently sitting in your cabinet. With respect and appreciation for premade spice rubs, we believe that the coffee spice rub is something that you can put together yourself on demand, using fresh coffee and your favorite base rub in perfect harmony.

We love this method because it doesn't require you to buy something new; you can use any rub of your choice. You might want to use a cabinet classic or make use of a beloved family recipe. If you're looking for guidance, you can't go wrong with mixing together equal parts ground white pepper, garlic salt, onion powder, cumin, coarse sea salt (such as Maldon or Jacobsen), dried oregano, and unrefined brown sugar. Spice rubs are an intensely personal thing, often passed down through family chefs, and a matter of individual preference. We absolutely love this aspect of home cooking and have come up with a handy method that's adaptable to just about any spice rub in your kitchen (and in your heart). Use it on the protein of your choice. (Lean cuts of steak, tempeh, hearty fish such as salmon or swordfish, and chicken are all great choices.) Something especially beautiful and delicious happens when this rub is applied to grilled grass-fed steak, ideally sourced from a family farm or small production butcher shop. Mindful meat is like well-sourced coffee: it's not just more ethical—it's also more delicious. This recipe can easily be scaled up—start by doubling or tripling the amount of ground coffee used, and add the same number of spices and salt to taste.

Makes 15 grams (⅛ cup)—scale up recipe for a larger quantity

10 grams (a bit less than 1 tablespoon) prepared spice rub (see headnote)

5 grams whole bean coffee, ground medium-coarse (similar to the French Press Brewing Method on page 60 or the Clever Dripper Brewing Method on page 67)

RECIPE CONTINUES

1 ——— **Thoroughly mix the spice** rub and the coffee together. (Ratios and measurements here matter only a little bit—if you want to be more rustic with things, filling a little dish with your favorite spice rub, then covering that rub with ground coffee is a great visual guidepost.)

2 ——— **Store the mixture in** an airtight container until ready to use for up to 2 weeks.

CASCARA SHRUB

We've been fascinated by the use of shrubs in coffee over the last decade. From the Arabic word *sharab*, meaning "to drink," shrubs, or vinegar cordials, are a familiar cocktail component, but they take on a whole new meaning when used in a coffee context. Shrubs have traditionally been a way to preserve fruit and add fruity flavors to the bartender's arsenal without relying on having the fresh stuff on hand.

For our purposes, we're making a shrub using the fruitiest part of the coffee experience: cascara, the dried fruit cherry of the coffee plant (see page 131). Shrubs typically include fresh berries, but for this we're using dried cascara. To replicate the juiciness of fresh berries, we reconstitute the dried fruit with equal parts water before adding the sugar. You'll wind up with a caffeinated, fruity, delicious drink that's beautiful either on its own with a splash of soda water or employed in a wide range of cocktails.

Makes 28 ounces

150 grams (10 tablespoons or 5 ounces) raw cascara

150 mL (⅔ cup) water

250 grams (1 cup) sugar, plus more to taste

250 mL (1 cup) apple cider vinegar

1 ——— **Place the cascara in** a 1-quart container with lid.

2 ——— **Add the water.**

3 ——— **Shake, shake, shake!**

4 ——— **Add the sugar.**

5 ——— **Shake, shake, shake!**

6 ——— **Cover and let the** mixture rest for 24 hours on your countertop (or in a dark, cool place away from sunlight). Shake occasionally (once before you go to bed, once when you wake up, and once every 4 to 6 hours in between). Make sure to keep the lid tight.

RECIPE CONTINUES

7 ——— **Strain the cascara through** a fine-mesh sieve or cheesecloth into a bowl. Discard the solids.

8 ——— **Add the apple cider** vinegar to the cascara liquid and stir to combine. The mixture should be bright and acidic from the vinegar—but not too bright or too acidic—and sweet and syrupy from the cascara but not too sweet. Adjust with additional sugar or vinegar to taste. Transfer the shrub to a flip-top bottle (for convenience and because it has a rubber seal to help maintain freshness). It will keep in your fridge for up to 6 months.

CASCARA SODA

1 ——— **Add 30 mL (2 tablespoons)** Cascara Shrub to a highball glass filled with ice.

2 ——— **Top with good-quality soda** water, like La Croix. Alternatively, use a sparkling mineral water such as Gerolsteiner or Borjomi for a creamy version of the drink.

Cascara

Roasted coffee beans are actually the seed of the coffee fruit. So where does all the fruit go? Truth is, a coffee cherry has very little "fruit" mucilage, and when coffee is processed, the peel, husk, and fruit are generally considered waste by-products of coffee and usually composted or discarded.

But in coffee-growing countries like Bolivia, Yemen, and Somalia, the fruit of coffee has been dried and used as an herbal tisane for centuries. Cascara goes by many names—in Yemen it's referred to as *qishr*, in Bolivia it's *sultana*, and in Somalia, *bun*. High-end specialty coffee growers like Aida Batlle of El Salvador have been pioneering elevated cascara production—with an eye for keeping toxins and pests at bay—for consumption throughout the world. In some cases, the price of cascara has eclipsed prices of green coffee! And delicious cascara can now be purchased at fine coffee retailers around the world.

When steeped, the beverage can have a fruit-forward and herbaceous quality, depending on the coffee variety and overall quality. Lightly caffeinated, it's lovely on ice. Folks have taken this product and created sweetened syrups, sodas, shrubs, kombucha, and even cascara-infused spirits. Starbucks Coffee Company introduced a cascara syrup and line of cascara-infused drinks in 2017. New Deal Distillery of Portland, Oregon, makes a cascara liqueur, and Good Liquorworks of New York's Finger Lakes region produces a cascara vodka.

To brew cascara at home, combine 20 grams of it in a liter of water (heated to 180°F or 82°C) and steep for 5 minutes.

COFFEE FLOWER TEA

Like cascara, coffee flower water uses a commonly discarded part of
the coffee plant and puts it to beautiful use. A kind of herbal tisane
made using hot water and coffee flowers has been known for centuries
in coffee-growing communities, but it's only recently that coffee
consumers in the United States, Europe, and Australia have had access
to this product.

Coffee trees (or treelets) naturally produce beautiful flowers as
part of their germination cycle. These flowers can be quite aromatic and
distinct, with notes of jasmine and honeysuckle. Enterprising farmers such as
Pedro Rodriguez of Caranavi, Bolivia, have developed a growing market
for their coffee flowers, partnering with roasting companies like Market Lane
Coffee of Melbourne, Australia, to sell and brew this distinct drink.

To be clear: these flowers are not roasted like conventional coffee. Instead
they're sun-dried on raised beds and then steeped as you would a good tea
or herbal tisane.

You can also enjoy this over ice in a highball glass or freeze the brew
into ice-pop molds (a wonderful treat on days when the temp is climbing
high). A splash of this flower tea in your next gin-and-tonic session is also a
welcome addition, particularly with an aromatic, floral, high-quality gin.

Makes 1 medium pot of tea
4 grams (1 teaspoon) dried coffee flowers
220 mL (not quite 1 cup) water heated to 176°F (80°C), which
    is just before boiling

1 ——— **Start with your favorite** teapot, glass server, or sizable
brewing vessel. A small Chemex works great here if that's your
preference.

2 ——— **Pour the hot water** over the coffee flowers and start a timer set
for 2 minutes. Allow the flowers to steep the full amount of time,
then decant the brewed tea from your vessel—don't over-steep
the flowers.

ZACHARY'S PERFECT COLD BREW TIRAMISU

Tiramisu—from *tirami su*, Italian for "pick me up"—is the most iconic coffee dessert on this or any planet. Chances are you've come across a few renditions over the years. Like many of coffee's most iconic beverages and foodstuffs, tiramisu's history and origins are widely disputed. We know it's from Italy, was invented in the twentieth century, and likely hails from the area around Venice known as Friuli Venezia Giulia.

Essential to the magic of the tiramisu is the use of coffee-dipped ladyfingers, a type of cakey-cookie that can be made at home or bought at a store (some swear by the latter). There are a great many adaptations of this dessert, and quite a few of those include alcohol as part of the build (typically Marsala sweet wine or Amaretto). But at least one very old recipe, from the restaurant Le Beccherie in Treviso, is alcohol-free. It's from this recipe, developed in 1969 by Alba di Pillo, that we're setting forth to tinker. We believe that the secret to elevating this dish is to use cool, concentrated coffee of a high quality: namely, our very own version of cold brew, following the recipe on page 80.

Note: When it comes to ladyfinger cookies, there are degrees of softness and hardness. You want a hard finger—or a soft finger that has been left out to grow a bit stale—which can gently absorb the coffee yet maintain girth and rigidity after dunking.

Makes 1 (8×8-inch) pan (serves 12)

2 large eggs, separated

67 grams (⅓ cup) sugar

227 grams (8 ounces) mascarpone cheese

Pinch of salt

240 mL (1 cup) Cold Brew (see page 80)

1 7-ounce (200-gram) package ladyfingers (see Note)

Unsweetened cocoa powder, for dusting

1 ——— **In a medium bowl,** beat the egg yolks and sugar with a hand mixer until the mixture is pale yellow and thick (3 minutes should do it).

2 ——— **Gently fold in** the mascarpone.

3 ——— **In a separate bowl,** beat the egg whites with a hand mixer on low speed. Add a pinch of salt and beat until stiff peaks form, about 3 minutes.

4 ——— **Fold the egg whites** into the bowl with the yolk-sugar-cheese mixture.

5 ——— **Pour the cold brew** into a shallow bowl large enough to submerge the ladyfingers. Gently dip the cookies in one at a time for a few seconds, just enough to soak in some cold brew without losing their cookie integrity. Transfer roughly half of the dunked cookies to the baking dish, touching and side by side, until you have a single layer of cookies on the bottom. Smooth half of the mascarpone mixture over the top. Repeat dunking the remaining cookies and placing them in the baking dish, then smooth another layer of the remaining mascarpone mixture on top.

6 ——— **Dust the top with** cocoa powder.

7 ——— **Carefully tent the dish** with foil, being mindful not to let the foil touch the top of the tiramisu. Place it in the refrigerator to chill for at least 4 hours. This time in the refrigerator is essential for the tiramisu to set, allowing all the ingredients to get to know each other.

8 ——— **Serve in rectangular slices** on a plate. Your tiramisu is good for up to 3 days in the fridge, but it will not last that long.

Chapter 6

IT'S FINALLY COCKTAIL HOUR

Since the dawn of time (or thereabouts), humankind has sought to fuse two great passions—coffee and mixology—into a unified, beautiful form. The coffee cocktail is nothing new, but each successive generation of coffee-and-cocktail lovers has sought to innovate within its hallowed concepts, looking back and forward in equal measure, to make the coffee cocktail their very own.

The production and consumption of fermented beverages date back to the Neolithic era, roughly 10,000 BCE; humans have consumed coffee cherries since at least the eighth century CE, and the brewing of what we would today recognize as "coffee" began in Ethiopia and Yemen around the 1500s. Interestingly, there's no hard-and-fast date on the "first" coffee cocktail or coffee liqueur. The brand Tia Maria claims that its secret recipe dates back to a seventeenth-century Jamaican coffee plantation, but this is quite likely a marketing claim. Jerry Thomas, the patron saint of pre-Prohibition cocktail culture, offers a recipe for a "Coffee Cocktail" in his seminal *Bar-Tender's Guide* (published in 1862), but the drink contains no actual coffee, instead relying on cognac, port, 1 whole egg, and nutmeg to produce a drink that simply *looks* like a cup of coffee. (Read on for an updated version with coffee at last included.)

Coffee cocktails exploded in the middle of the twentieth century, spurred on by the invention of the Irish Coffee (by Joe Sheridan in 1943), the widespread distribution of popular coffee liqueurs including Tia Maria and Kahlúa, and the increasing popularity of coffee consumption as a daily drink for millions worldwide, led by iconic brands like Folgers and Café Bustelo. It's in this mid-century collision moment when we get drinks like the White Russian, the Espresso Martini, and the Coffee Nudge, each with its own long-enduring narrative (and surprising continued popularity).

Today, much of modern cocktail culture is focused on the pursuit of quality, originality, and inclusivity, and for lovers of the coffee cocktail, it's never been a better time to imbibe—even if you don't partake in alcohol itself. We're living in a golden age of zero-proof mixology, a concept that captures the fun and convivial nature of cocktail culture with the alcohol kindly set aside. Zero-proof cocktails are a particularly exciting avenue for coffee drinks; coffee is such a profoundly complex beverage, as we've learned in previous pages, and as a plaything for a creative bartender, it can be used with marvelous impact.

We've found coffee cocktails we love all over the world, including, yes, the espresso martini, which has enjoyed renewed vigor and vogue over the last few years, thanks in no small part to its public consumption by thirsty and eager celebrities. But a wonderful world of coffee cocktails beyond this waits to be explored and many keen and clever ways to enjoy the mixological arts without the use of spirits. Of all the wonderful things coffee is capable of, its place at the heart of your home bar is perhaps the most impressive of all.

So come with us—it's happy hour, after all! Let down your hair a bit, unbutton that collar—or unzip your Patagonia shell, whatever—and let's delve into the cocktail hour, for which the implied entendre of "drinking coffee" can be served at last.

"We think about coffee as seasoning, an ingredient. I encourage you to play with your coffee at home away from judgment and criticism. Everyone's palate is completely different, and there're so many ways to make coffee, and so many different ways to think about how to combine it with other delicious elements."

—Daniel Brown

The Espresso Martini: A Brief History

No coffee cocktail has enjoyed a more meteoric rise to popularity here in the twenty-first century than the espresso martini. Thanks to a rash of celebrity fans (Larry David, Timothée Chalamet) and prominent placements at buzzy cocktail bars, consumption of the espresso martini rose more than 300 percent year over year in the first part of the 2020s —*Vogue* dubbed it "the cocktail for our times," the British edition of *GQ* published an extensive oral history of the drink's origin story, and *New York Magazine* called it "the hottest drink on the planet."

There's no denying the cocktail's populist appeal nor its unique ability to simultaneously defog and uplift those who partake in its charms. Still, you more or less could have knocked us over with a feather when the espresso martini zeitgeist began to take hold; we remember encountering it in slightly different circumstances in London, where the drink was invented in the early 1980s and never really went away. In London, the espresso martini has for decades remained a mainstay at party-hearty bars and cheeky restaurants with modern art collections, occupying a place similar to the vodka Red Bull in America: a drink built to do a job, synonymous with late nights out drinking and making poor decisions. Drinking dodgy espresso martinis—sticky-sweet with too much liqueur and garnished with floating burnt beans—in London a decade ago, we would have never guessed this drink would be so wildly popular someday in America, much less that we'd be writing about it in this book. But here's the thing: done well, an espresso martini is *delicious*, and it serves as a neat entry point for us to talk about the many ways coffee can be employed at the home bar.

A very classic version of an espresso martini in a busy cocktail setting would include bar standards like Smirnoff or Stoli for the vodka, ubiquitous and beloved Kahlúa for the liqueur, and a shot of espresso from the bar's commercial espresso machine. We would wager that the vast majority of espresso martinis made and served at bars worldwide follow this format quite closely.

A more upscale version of an espresso martini at a craft-focused cocktail bar might start with a smaller production artisan vodka, such as that made by Barr Hill of Vermont or Belvedere of Poland. Most craft distilleries in the gin, eau de vie, or brandy trade also make vodka, and chances are there's a good one near where you live—bartenders tend to be quite opinionated on this subject, we've found. From there, the craft cocktail bar might choose to fancy up their choice of coffee liqueur, with brands like Mr Black (Australia) and St. George (California) producing outstanding craft coffee spirits. Last, this quality-focused cocktail bar will already have a relationship with an excellent reputable coffee company, so the coffee component will be sourced via that partnership. This might mean it's a smart, complex shot of espresso from the cocktail bar's well-maintained espresso machine (the best possible scenario), but it could also suggest they're using a purpose-made concentrate or cold brew (we've seen this out at bars a lot as well). The truth is the "espresso" component of an espresso martini is more taxonomic than prescriptive.

The espresso martini is built like so many classic cocktails in that it is a simple combination of three distinct ingredients plus ice. But every single inch of the espresso martini can (and should!) be tweaked, fussed with, and dialed in to your liking. At home you can play with ratios, employ your own homemade Coffee Vodka (see page 146) or a splash of your own Cold Brew (see page 80).

You might have a special soft spot in your heart for one of the classic coffee liqueurs, like Tia Maria, or feel strongly that the all-consuming singular flavor of Kahlúa is actually a required component in the espresso martini build, sort of like a Jack & Coke simply has to be made with Jack Daniels and Coca-Cola. If you've gone the espresso-machine-at-home-route (see chapter 4), this is one of your best-use test cases—there are few things more impressive in an entertaining setting than whipping up a batch of espresso martinis at home using real espresso. And you can always make swaps and substitutions on a whim—using concentrated coffee rather than espresso, adding a dash of real cream, swapping mezcal for vodka, reaching for the top-shelf Patrón coffee liqueur, or playing up the drink's smooth coldness by batching and freezing the entire thing ahead of time. (Just be sure to give it a good shake before serving.)

For all these reasons, we like thinking about the espresso martini as a building block for making delicious coffee cocktails at home. There are so many ways you can go with it, and that's really part of the fun. That's why we offer not one but three recipes for making a killer great espresso martini at home. These recipes are categorized as Classic, Classy, and the Sprudge Original—the last recipe is quite controversial, but we think the results are extraordinary.

"Concentrated Coffee"

A note on "concentrated coffee": We do not *necessarily* mean a coffee concentrate as it is popularly understood. Here we are instead referring to *strength*, that nebulous, much-abused term in the coffee industry that sometimes refers to roast level, sometimes refers to caffeine content, and sometimes refers to a cup of coffee's total dissolved solids. We're using "concentrated coffee" to imply that you want either a shot of espresso or something reminiscent of a shot of espresso, which might be a concentrated instant coffee (cut the amount of water by three-fourths) or, in a pinch, the use of a cold brew concentrate.

CLASSIC ESPRESSO MARTINI

This is the most common version of an espresso martini, and it's quite similar to what you'll find at most bars that serve the drink. A lot of vodka, a little bit of coffee, a readily available liqueur, lots of shaking over ice, and boom—you've got a coffee cocktail drink that's captured the public's imagination.

Makes 1 martini

2.5 ounces (4¾ tablespoons) vodka, stored in the freezer

1 double shot of espresso (1.5 ounces, or 3 tablespoons)

1 ounce (2 tablespoons) Kahlúa

3 whole coffee beans, for garnish

1 —— **Combine the liquid ingredients** in a cocktail shaker and shake with ice.

2 —— **Strain into a freezing-cold** martini coupe (see Note). Serve immediately with 3 coffee beans on top.

NOTE: We love using smaller martini coupes, as a traditional martini would have been served a hundred years ago. But of course if you've got one of those severe angular numbers you like to use when making a Cosmo, this is absolutely the perfect time to bust it out. Pro tip: For an extra-chilly touch, try freezing your glassware for an hour before you make your drinks.

CLASSY ESPRESSO MARTINI

Allow us to up the ante a bit here by using premium ingredients at every step. Contrary to popular belief, vodka is *not* all created equal, and very good, very cold, imported vodka like the kinds we're recommending makes a vast world of difference in every place you use it. The same is true for the espresso you use, and it also carries over to the coffee liqueur in your espresso martini. Kahlúa is a beloved cocktail bar mainstay for good reason, but it's also not the end of the conversation as far as coffee liqueurs go. We've got a few to recommend below, but you should also consider exploring and experimenting with options from a local distillery near you.

Makes 1 martini

2.5 ounces (4¾ tablespoons) of very, very cold imported vodka, such as Effen, Belvedere, or Chopin

1 double shot of espresso (1.5 ounces, or 3 tablespoons) made using a washed arabica blend, sourced from an excellent roaster such as Onyx Coffee, Stumptown Coffee, or Joe Coffee

1 ounce (2 tablespoons) of Mr Black Cold Brew Coffee Liqueur or St. George Spirits NOLA Coffee Liqueur

3 whole coffee beans, for garnish

1 ——— **Combine the liquid ingredients** in a cocktail shaker and shake with ice.

2 ——— **Strain into a freezing-cold** martini coupe (see Note on page 142) and serve immediately with 3 beans on top. Shake up a second batch posthaste before the Lyft arrives.

SPRUDGE ESPRESSO MARTINI

In a book full of recipes, this is one we're especially in love with, and we implore you to give it a try. At its core, the espresso martini is a union of four pillars: coffee, sugar, alcohol, and agitation. In traditional formulations, the alcohol comes from a neutral vodka, and the sugar and coffee flavoring come via both a coffee liqueur and a shot of espresso, with agitation provided at the very end via a vigorous ice shake. But you're not required to stick to any of these rules: there is no dogma in coffee and even less when it comes to the wild world of espresso martinis. And so we started playing.

First we wanted to introduce our beautiful Coffee Vodka from page 146—this is wonderful tasting and smelling stuff, and it's also quite malleable—a ready friend for many cocktail builds. Combined with a shot of espresso, you'll have plenty of coffee flavor, but how about the sugar? Well—between the coffee vodka and the coffee itself, perhaps that makes the liqueur overkill? The truth is many coffee liqueurs tend to dominate the drinks that feature them. So we went in a different direction, introducing port, a fortified wine from Portugal. Add a good firm shake—30 seconds up and down with plenty of ice—to produce the creamy texture and iconic foamy "head" that espresso martini drinkers love. Your drink won't be noticeably purple or anything from the port, but it will have more fruit presence, drawing out some of the floral and fruity flavors from your delicious shot of espresso.

> Makes 1 martini
>
> 2.5 ounces (⅓ cup) Incredibly Good Homemade Coffee Vodka (page 146)
>
> 1 double shot of espresso (1.5 ounces, or 3 tablespoons)
>
> 1 ounce (1 tablespoon) port wine
>
> 3 whole coffee beans, for garnish

1 —— **Combine the liquid ingredients** in a cocktail shaker. Shake vigorously with ice.

2 —— **Strain into a freezing-cold** martini coupe (see Note on page 142) and serve immediately with 3 beans on top.

A Note on Port

As with most things in life and beverages, there are many different routes one can choose when it comes to the port in this recipe. It's perhaps wise to suggest that you use whatever you've got on hand: tawny port, ruby port, or even a nice, crusted port will all do wonders. Port is marvelous stuff! One might even try subbing in white port, which yields a different and no less delightful flavor profile. For us, there's nothing finer than a good vintage port made by one of the venerable old houses like Cockburn's, Taylor Fladgate, Graham's, or Dow's. A nice bottle of port works wonders in this cocktail, but it's also quite a happy sidecar addition to your next cheese plate.

INCREDIBLY GOOD HOMEMADE COFFEE VODKA

We know flavored vodka gets a bad rap. Vodka in general has long been the subject of derision among a certain subset of so-called sophisticated twenty-first-century drinkers for whom flavored vodka is even more of an eye-roll supreme.

But hear us out. As with many nodes of contemporary snobbery, this perception does not tell the whole story. Good, thoughtfully made flavored vodka can be absolutely delicious, and if you've cast this stuff out of your repertoire as the exclusive domain of college frat bars and Flirtini cosmos, it's really time to reconsider.

We were not always this enlightened. What changed us was having the opportunity to try flavored vodka's culinary possibilities by way of a restaurant here in Portland, Oregon, called Kachka, a municipal gem focused on the culinary traditions of Russia and Eastern Europe through the lens of the Ashkenazi Jewish diaspora. At Kachka, the bar program is focused on vodka in a big way, and Kachka's flavored vodkas are truly a revelation: expressive, moreish, and profoundly culinary, conveying traditional Eastern European flavors like bison grass, horseradish, tarragon, and caraway, alongside Pacific Northwest seasonal expressions like Chester blackberries and Mt. Hood strawberries. We felt inspired to work on something bespoke and homemade in the style of these and have developed a tried-and-true home coffee vodka technique with roughly 1 million potential applications for the finished product, not least of which being an ice-cold shot straight from the freezer for each of your guests at the start of brunch.

Makes 1 (375 mL) bottle

1 bottle (375 mL) Monopolowa vodka (or vodka of choice; see Note on page 148)

20 grams (0.71 ounce) roasted whole bean coffee

10 grams (2⅓ teaspoons) Okinawa black sugar (see Note on page 148)

RECIPE CONTINUES

1 ——— **Pour the vodka into** a pitcher. There it will rest awaiting further instructions.

2 ——— **Add your roasted coffee** beans directly into the empty vodka bottle and add the sugar on top.

3 ——— **Slowly return the vodka** to the vodka bottle. Adding coffee and sugar into the bottle means it'll hold less liquid, so fill it up nearly to the top, then do what you wish with the shot or so of the remaining vodka—a splash into tonight's pasta sauce, perhaps, or straight down the hatch.

4 ——— **Place the bottle in** your liquor cabinet—beans and all—and set a timer for 72 hours.

5 ——— **When that time is** up, pour the infused vodka back into the original transfer vessel. (It's easy enough to do this without the beans spilling into the vessel, but if one or two sneak by, simply scoop them out using a slotted spoon.) Give your 375 mL bottle a good rinse and discard the coffee beans.

6 ——— **Once the bottle is** clean and clear, transfer the vodka back into the original bottle, give it a good wipe for any excess liquid, and toss that sucker into the side bin of your freezer for future employment.

A NOTE ON VODKA: A broad spectrum of vodka expressions and prices exists, from special-edition offerings from Poland and Russia that retail well above $100 to bottom-shelf plastic bottle affairs. For our purposes, Monopolowa of Poland does nicely.

A NOTE ON COFFEE: After you attempt several batches, it'll be clear that your finished vodka will ever-so-slightly take on the unique characteristics of whatever coffee you chose to infuse it with. Maybe use your favorite everyday drinking blend; maybe use a rare Gesha or Wush-Wush or what have you. The choice is yours.

A NOTE ON SUGAR: Speaking molecularly for a moment, sugar greatly helps the botanical infusion process when making coffee vodka, and it also results in an agreeably off-dry final product. Just trust me on this one: without sugar, coffee's oils and esters wind up clashing with the vodka, with a result that tastes like someone spilled a diner mug into a bottle of nail polish remover. Please also trust us on the Okinawa black sugar, which has a salted caramel flavor profile and helps give your infusion a fine bit of backbone. Find this sugar online or at your local Asian specialty food store.

Consider Irish Coffee

We absolutely adore Irish coffee; just between us, this is the *real* coffee cocktail GOAT, and it deserves some of the modern zeitgeist shine and praise currently being lavished on the espresso martini.

It's quite likely based on a few different Viennese cafe society cocktails popularized around the turn of the twentieth century, in particular the Fiaker, in which sweetened espresso was topped with foam then floated with kirschwasser or plum brandy. A military coffee shop in rural County Clare is allegedly where the modern Irish coffee was invented in 1943, by a guy called Joe Sheridan; the recipe was then brought to America by the *San Francisco Chronicle* drinks and travel writer Stanton Delaplane, who perfected the recipe at the iconic Buena Vista cafe near Fisherman's Wharf. In the decades since then, Buena Vista has served more than 30 million orders of its signature Irish coffees, including a not-insignificant number to the authors of this book.

There's something glorious about the simplicity of the Buena Vista's Irish coffee in which each component is given pride of place: a glass goblet containing medium-roasted coffee, Tullamore D.E.W. Irish whiskey, cubed sugar, and a thick layer of heavy whipping cream floated on top, almost like the foamy head of a Guinness beer. The coffee dissolves the sugar, melds with the whiskey, and then is drunk straight through the head of cool cream to marvelous effect.

The world is full of sad, bad Irish coffees, with sugar, dark roast, and whiskey slopped together in a diner mug, and this is *not* the sort of Irish coffee tradition we want any part of. At the same time, the Irish coffee as served at Buena Vista is not the last word on the drink's form and function, and for a lovely Irish coffee at home, we (unsurprisingly) have a few suggestions.

The most important thing is actually the cream: it should be heavy whipping cream, which you then lightly aerate using a hand-held frother or, even better, an upright blender. (You can also vigorously whisk by hand in a pinch, but stop before the cream forms peaks.) The second most important thing is the glass: a 6-inch glass tulip is perfect, and it's handy to keep in your kitchen cabinets, as they are also perfect for serving ice cream sundaes.

We offer two recipes for the Irish coffee at home, one quite traditional and one built for those who prefer a zero-proof experience. A proper zero-proof Irish coffee is much more than just cream atop sweetened coffee; it actually takes some thought and consideration and in the right hands is every bit as delicious and memorable as its tipsy counterpart.

MOSTLY CLASSIC IRISH COFFEE

Our two big departures here are the whiskey and the sugar.
Tullamore D.E.W. is a fine whiskey, no doubt, but the category of
Irish whiskey is deep, and there are perhaps more characteristic and
evocative offerings being distilled today on the island. Green Spot,
in particular, takes an Irish coffee in unexpected directions, as
though the whole thing has been spiked pleasantly with a bit of spiced
apple, and Knappogue Castle's entry-level 12-year is worth nipping neat
between the whirring whipped-cream buzz of the blender.

As for the sugar, well—sugar and coffee have a lot in common.
They are commodity products with a deeply impactful and at times quite dark
colonial history, which most people don't really think twice about, and there's
quite a lot to say about how different styles and traditions of sugar impact
the end flavor of so many foods and drinks we love. A dark, caramel-toned,
complex Demerara sugar simple syrup is your friend for so many cocktail
builds, like the ti' punch or a traditional daiquiri, but try swapping some in for
the plain white sugar cube more typically found in an Irish coffee. We think
the results take the drink up a notch of quantum complexity.

Makes 1 drink

Hot water heated to 180°F (82°C) for preheating the glass

Splash of Demerara Simple Syrup (recipe follows)

4 ounces (½ cup) hot filter coffee (ideally a daily drinking
blend from your favorite roaster)

2 ounces (¼ cup) Irish whiskey (Tullamore D.E.W. is
traditional, but we also like Knappogue Castle, Green
Spot, and Writers' Tears)

Frothed cool cream, in the style of Buena Vista (see sidebar)

1 ——— **Preheat your glass with** the hot water—fill it nearly to the
top, and allow it to sit for at least 30 seconds to fully warm the
vessel. Ideally, you're using a traditional Irish coffee tulip, but any
heatproof 6-ounce glass will do.

2 ——— **Discard the preheating water,** then add a splash of Demerara Simple Syrup to the heated glass.

3 ——— **Add the coffee, then** pour the whiskey.

4 ——— **Gently, carefully, with a** practiced hand, float a layer of frothed cool cream on top of the drink. Serve immediately.

DEMERARA SIMPLE SYRUP

Makes 12 ounces
1 cup demerara sugar
1 cup water

1 ——— **Add the sugar to** a small saucepan. Pour 1 cup of water over, then bring to a boil over high heat. Reduce the heat and simmer, stirring occasionally, for 5 minutes.

2 ——— **Allow to cool completely,** then store in a bottle or flask with a sealed lid. It will keep for 1 month in the refrigerator.

The Tricky Part

The cream-float bit at the end is tricky, to the consternation of bartenders worldwide, but a few tips can work wonders. First, do not overwhip your cream—you don't really want "whipped cream," but rather a lightly frothed cream. Next, consider using the back of a metal spoon when pouring the cream, which will slow down the pour and create an even, unbroken layer of cream and coffee. The drink should appear "sealed," with no frothy cream dropping down into the coffee. We've also seen folks use a plastic squeeze bottle, which gives you additional control over the pour—this is how they do it at Tom Bergin's in Los Angeles, home to a truly excellent Irish coffee.

SPRUDGE ZERO-PROOF IRISH COFFEE

It seems like this should be such a no-brainer, but even the famous places get it wrong. Let us shout it from the rooftops: a zero-proof Irish coffee is *not* just coffee, sugar, and cream. Here's how we like to make ours.

We are, of course, aware of the exploding world of spirit analogs but have never tried one that quite works for this drink. Instead we like making a concoction using a short, tight, shotlike amount of over-steeped black tea derived from Assamica. (While any English Breakfast tea will do, a Tippy Assam from India or Sri Lanka is best for maximum effect.) Over-steeped black tea helps create a tightened mouthfeel and woody secondary flavor tone for this drink, which, when blended with the sugar, coffee, and cream, evokes a classic Irish coffee mouthfeel and flavor quite effectively.

Makes 1 drink

Water heated to 180°F (82°C), for preheating the glass

Splash of Demerara Simple Syrup (page 151)

4 ounces (½ cup) hot filter coffee (ideally a daily drinking blend from your favorite roaster)

2 ounces (¼ cup) over-steeped black tea (see page 153)

Frothed cool cream (see page 151)

1 ——— **Preheat your Irish coffee** glass with the hot water—fill it nearly to the top and allow it to sit for at least 30 seconds to fully warm the vessel. Ideally, you're using a traditional Irish coffee tulip, but any heatproof 6-ounce glass will do.

2 ——— **Discard the preheating water,** then add a splash of demerara syrup to the bottom of the heated glass.

3 ——— **Add the hot coffee,** then pour the oversteeped tea on top.

4 ——— **Gently, carefully, with a** practiced hand, float a layer of frothed cool cream on top of the drink. Serve immediately.

A Note on Steeping Tea

Over-steeping your tea is a central part of this cocktail, and we played with it a ton in our test kitchen. There are several approaches you might choose to take, depending on what tea you have on hand. (Most folks have a couple of bags of tea rattling around the cupboards, and it's absolutely fine to use those.) Start with 2 tea bags to 4 ounces (½ cup) of boiling hot water, and steep for 5 minutes. You'll wind up with a tight, puckery, rather unpleasant brew, but don't fret—it works beautifully in the finished cocktail. But if you're tea geeks like we are (we actually, really, really love tea, despite this being, you know, a coffee book), then maybe you've got something a little more distinct to brew with, like a nice smoky Lapsang souchong or some strong, slightly fermented pu-erh, or even a Tippy Assam from India or Sri Lanka. All of these styles of tea work beautifully in this cocktail. To over-steep them, simply double the amount of tea you would usually use for a 4-ounce cup. For example, 10 grams of tea to 6 ounces of boiling water at 5 minutes' brew time is a solid ratio to create the over-steeped effect you're looking for, but this can be tweaked and refined, depending on the specific tea you're working with.

Note that for all the over-steeps, we suggest you brew with 6 ounces (¾ cup) of water, which yields enough over-steeped tea to make two Zero-Proof Irish Coffees. This can be easily scaled up if you're entertaining or planning on enjoying several of these delicious drinks yourself. As the bartender once told us at the Buena Vista, "Irish Coffees don't start getting good until you've had three."

Espresso and Sparkling Wine

One of the simplest coffee cocktails in this book isn't really a cocktail at all but rather a suggested pairing, one that draws on the very old tradition of serving a shot of espresso with sparkling water. Somewhere along the way the inspiration struck us: Why not serve a perfect shot of espresso alongside a beautiful glass of sparkling wine?

The elegance of this pairing is matched only by the effectiveness: these drinks taste *beautiful* together, warping and wending in a dance of complexity, amplifying each other in strange and meaningful ways. The choice of espresso impacts the choice of wine, and vice versa, but before we go too deeply into suggested pairings, it's preferable to start with what you know best. If there's a favorite sparkling wine in your fridge, use that. If you're fortunate enough to have a favorite style of sparkling wine—like, say, Champagne—this is a fun new wrinkle to appreciate it even more. And if you're brand-new to sparkling wine, start with something affordable from your local wine shop. (Feel free to ask the wine shop staff for ideas.)

From there this pairing is a blank canvas to play with. There's no *one* kind of sparkling wine—any nation on earth that makes wine also makes sparkling wine, and every last version is a unique expression. From much happy experimenting, here are five combinations we've come to really love.

⚡ **Stumptown Hair Bender Espresso**
with Roederer Estate Brut

⚡ **Blue Bottle Coffee Guatemala El Injerto Single Origin Espresso**
with Case Paolin Asolo Prosecco Col Fondo

⚡ **Verve Streetlevel All-Purpose Espresso**
with Donkey & Goat Lily's Pet Nat sparkling wine

⚡ **Equator Coffees Tigerwalk Espresso**
with Sea Smoke Sea Spray sparkling wine

⚡ **Tim Wendelboe Nacimiento Espresso**
with Stroebel Champagne Triptyque

CASCARA COBBLER

This is a wicked good riff on the classic Sherry Cobbler cocktail, a recipe that dates back to the popularization of ice cubes on demand in the early decades of the nineteenth century. The Sherry Cobbler is a simple combination of Spanish sherry wine, sugar, and citrus, mixed over plentiful ice in a long, tall glass, and often topped with aromatic herbs such as mint, rosemary, or lime leaf. It's a drink with vast influence in the pantheon of cocktails and, indeed, is credited for helping popularize the drinking straw, thanks in no small part to its name-check in Charles Dickens's *The Life and Adventures of Martin Chuzzlewit* (1842–1844). Our vision subs in a delicious cascara simple syrup (recipe follows) in place of the Sherry Cobbler's more typical use of plain white sugar. After some experimentation, we're happy to suggest the use of amontillado sherry in the crafting of this drink, such as that offered by Lustau or Gonzales Byass.

Makes 1 drink

1 ounce (2 teaspoons) Cascara Simple Syrup (recipe follows)

1 lemon wheel

1 orange wheel

4 ounces (½ cup) amontillado sherry

Crushed ice or pebble ice

Aromatic herbs, such as mint sprig, lime leaf, or rosemary,
    for garnish

1 ——— **Muddle the simple syrup** with the lemon and orange wheels in the bottom of a cocktail shaker. Pour the sherry directly over the top, add ice cubes, and shake with force and pep.

2 ——— **Strain the drink into** a tall, proud highball glass filled with fluffy crushed ice (or pebble ice if you have it), adding more crushed ice to the top of the drink after filling. Hoist mint or other fresh herbs atop the beverage, then plunge a straw down to its chilly depths. Drink immediately!

BREW TIP: Consider doubling the amount of citrus used to amp up the brighter tones of this drink, perfect for a hot summer's day.

RECIPE CONTINUES

CASCARA SIMPLE SYRUP

Makes 200 mL (a bit more than ¾ cup)
250 mL (1 cup) brewed cascara (see page 131)
250 grams (1 cup) sugar

1 ——— **Combine the brewed cascara** and sugar in a heavy-bottomed saucepan set over medium-high heat.

2 ——— **Bring the mixture to** a boil, then reduce the heat to low and simmer for 5 minutes, stirring constantly.

3 ——— **Decant the mixture into** a heatproof container with a lid (but do not cover it yet) and allow it to cool.

4 ——— **Once cooled, seal the** container and place it in the refrigerator. The cascara syrup will keep for up to 1 month.

BREW TIP: This syrup tastes brilliant in your Cascara Cobbler, but don't stop there—try adding a splash to an Amaro Nonino and soda, or shake it with ice, lime juice, and rum for an uplifting daiquiri. It's also absolutely delicious on its own over rocks with club soda or as a bright addition to the coffee syrup shaved ice mentioned on page 114.

UPDATED JERRY THOMAS COFFEE COCKTAIL
(NOW WITH 100% MORE COFFEE)

The Jerry Thomas Coffee Cocktail (from Thomas's seminal 1862 *Bar-Tender's Guide*) is infamous for *not* actually containing coffee; instead, the drink is meant to evoke the feeling of drinking a spiked coffee, through a delicious fusion of cognac, ruby port, Demerara simple syrup, and one whole egg, yolk and all.

Now, in the 160 years since it was invented, widespread availability of coffee has grown by roughly 1 million percent; conversely, our societal impulse to drink an entire raw egg in the course of a cocktail hour has significantly gone down. Like a lot of the lesser-remembered drinks in the *Bar-Tender's Guide*, the Coffee Cocktail is kind of weird—they can't all be Manhattans.

And so, allow us to provide a gentle update to the Jerry Thomas Coffee Cocktail of yester-yesteryear, now crafted with the inclusion of delicious coffee and only egg whites, setting aside the yolk instead perhaps for the crafting of our delicious Coffee Custard on page 124.

To make this drink pop, we like to combine the 1.5 ounces of cognac with whole coffee beans and let it rest for 24 hours before serving. A simple ratio of 10 grams of coffee per every 1.5 ounces of cognac works perfectly, and it can be scaled up if you enjoy the results. A natural processed coffee is especially well-suited to this drink.

Makes 1 drink

1.5 ounces (3 tablespoons) coffee-rested cognac (see above)

1.5 ounces (3 tablespoons) tawny port

0.5 ounce (1 tablespoon) Demerara Simple Syrup (see page 151)

1 large egg white

2 medium ice cubes

Splash of heavy cream or alternative milk of choice

Ground coffee and grated nutmeg, for garnish

1 ——— **Place all liquid ingredients** in a chilled Boston shaker without ice.

2 ——— **Give the full contents** a dry shake—with no ice—for 30 seconds.

3 ——— **Pop the top of** the shaker and add 2 medium ice cubes. Using a barspoon, stir the mixture gently for another 30 seconds to promote dilution.

4 ——— **Strain the mixture into** a Nick & Nora coupe or lowball cocktail glass, then top with a generous sprinkle of a 50/50 mixture of ground coffee and grated nutmeg.

SPRUDGE NUDGE

The Coffee Nudge is nothing special—you will not read rhapsodic endorsements of it in the annals of cocktail history, nor will you discover much in the way of whimsical reappraisals or mixological riffs. As far as we know, Timothée Chalamet has never been photographed drinking one.

But we think the Coffee Nudge is worth your time. It splits the difference in structure between an Irish coffee and an espresso martini—it looks more like the former but uses ingredients more like the latter. We love it not only as a catch-all place to play with the various delicious coffee tricks you now have at your at-home disposal but also because it's a drink without much in the way of hype or vibe, which means you are free to impart your own designs upon it.

A classic Coffee Nudge combines brandy, crème de cacao, and coffee liqueur with hot coffee in a tulip glass, the same type of vessel you'd serve Irish coffee in. And much like an Irish coffee, it should be topped with gently whipped cream (see page 151). In our Sprudge version, we are going to politely skip the crème de cacao in favor of a lovely homemade chocolate ganache (see page 163), and we're going to dial up the booze by going 50/50 brandy and our own homemade coffee vodka. Last, this is a great place to play with one of those interesting nouveau coffee liqueurs, like Mr Black or St. George. For the coffee component of this drink, we especially like the heavy mouthfeel of a French press brew (see page 62). This drink not only is lovely to sip at home but also makes a particularly welcome companion in a travel-ready thermos, perhaps for a snowy walk in the park.

Makes 1 drink

4 ounces (½ cup) French press coffee, using a filter coffee blend from your favorite roaster

1 ounce (2 tablespoons) brandy

1 ounce (2 tablespoons) Incredibly Good Homemade Coffee Vodka (see page 146)

0.5 ounce (1 tablespoon) of coffee liqueur, such as Mr Black or St. George

RECIPE CONTINUES

```
0.5 ounce (1 tablespoon) of homemade Chocolate Ganache
    (recipe follows)
Whipped cream (homemade or store-bought) for topping
    (a hearty plop)
Cocoa powder, for dusting (optional)
```

1 ——— **Combine all liquid ingredients** in a tulip glass and gently stir 5 times to incorporate.

2 ——— **Top with the whipped** cream. A dusting of cocoa powder atop the cream is not required, but it's recommended.

CHOCOLATE GANACHE

This ganache is also positively brilliant when used in a good homemade mocha (see page 102).

```
Makes 200 mL (a bit more than ¾ cup)
8 ounces (1 cup) dark chocolate (we like chocolate brands
    such as Dick Taylor, Askinosie, or Pump Street Chocolate)
125 grams (½ cup) of heavy cream
```

1 ——— **Roughly chop or break** apart the dark chocolate, and place it in a medium heatproof bowl.

2 ——— **In a medium saucepan,** heat the heavy cream on the stove over medium-high heat, until it comes to a gentle boil (3 to 4 minutes with a watchful eye).

3 ——— **Pour the heavy cream** directly over the chocolate and stir using a wooden spoon or spatula until the chocolate melts and the cream and the chocolate are incorporated.

4 ——— **Use the ganache immediately** for your Sprudge Nudge. You can store the remainder in an airtight container in the fridge for up to 1 week. It can be reheated using a double boiler or a cheeky zap in the microwave.

COFFEE HOT TODDY

There is no more comforting cold-weather drink known to beast or man than the hot toddy, a delightful tipple that owes much to a murky colonial past. The name "hot toddy" is adapted from the Indian word *taddy*, which refers to a very old technique of fermenting palm sap. Under colonial rule, traders began incorporating Indian spices and black tea into the British tradition of mixing Scotch whisky with hot water on cold, damp nights. It was a hit and took off in newspaper recipes around the world as a cure for the common cold.

There are quite literally thousands of riffs on the modern hot toddy, but most rely on a common bedrock combination of ingredients: spices, honey, black tea, Scotch, and hot water. Happily for us, this offers an easy flip into the realm of the coffee, utilizing the floral, herbal notes found in the highly prized arabica coffees of Kenya, brewed gently over an AeroPress to further enhance the tealike effect. Coffee and Scotch might seem like two opposing forces, but any conflict is happily overcome by the introduction of sweetness and spice; our recipe utilizes a bouquet of Indian spices in a nod to the hot toddy's original inspiration.

Note: You might notice that our Coffee Hot Toddy omits lemon, which is common in hot toddy drinks, and that's very much on purpose—we think that lemon flavors get a little clashy in a coffee cocktail like this one. However, while the addition of a dollop of whipped cream to this toddy is optional and far from traditional, it is highly recommended.

Makes 1 drink

2 ounces (¼ cup) peated single malt Scotch whisky (such as
    Ardbeg, Bunnahabhain, or Laphroaig)

1 teaspoon high-quality honey (we like to source ours locally
    and suggest you do the same)

1 cinnamon stick

3 ounces (¼ cup+2 teaspoons) coffee (ideally from Kenya,
    Tanzania, or Rwanda, when in season), AeroPress brewed
    (see page 53)

1 orange slice, studded with 3 whole cloves

2 dashes cardamom bitters

Dollop of whipped cream (optional)

1 —— **Add the Scotch to** your glass of choice. (A cider glass works great here, but your favorite coffee mug will do just fine as well.) Add the honey, then stir with the cinnamon stick to dissolve and incorporate them.

2 —— **Pour in the coffee,** stirring once more with the cinnamon stick. Add your clove-studded orange slice, then finish with dashes of cardamom bitters—and whipped cream (if using).

COFFEE NEGRONI

Negroni—its very utterance invokes the chicest aperitivo hour, with the promise of an evening's fabulous enjoyments ahead. But the drink's modern zeitgeist also owes a great deal to the endless permutations implied by the Negroni's simple structure: gin, vermouth, and Campari, poured in equal measure and stirred with ice, served over more ice with an orange garnish.

Nearly every portion of this combination is adjustable, tweakable, and endlessly interchangeable, save perhaps the Campari portion, which gives the Negroni its appealing sunset ochre hue and appetite-stirring bitter bite. For us, a Negroni needs Campari to truly earn its 'groni stripes; we are aware this declaration omits the drink known as the White Negroni, which makes use of ingredients like Lillet Blanc and Suze and is its own beast entirely.

The Mezcal Negroni, the Amaro Negroni, the Bermuda Negroni, the Negroni Sbagliato: all this and more awaits the thirsty and inventive bartender interested in tweaking the drink's infinitely riff-able baseline. Which brings us to this Coffee Negroni. Our version stays true to the founding spirit of the Negroni, which is to say it is a cocktail composed of gin, vermouth, and, of course, Campari, a wonderfully complex spirit that reminds us not a little bit of a good shot of washed espresso: bitter yet sweet, floral yet dry, redolent of fruit yet utterly expressive of its own identity.

As with any simple drink—and this is a deceptively simple one—the choice of which gin and which vermouth is very much part of the fun, as well as the ratios in which you intend to blend them. Read on for a road map on our favorite expression, after much tinkering. But let's give coffee pride of place here; this is Coffee Negroni, after all. Ultimately, in this drink we found coffee's home not in the spirits but in the ice: first stirring the drink with an ice cube made of Honduras La Cueva by Partners Coffee Roasters and then by serving the drink with another coffee cube, which will slowly dilute and subtly impart smart coffee flavors with each sip. In this way, the addition of brewed coffee is allowed to mingle with the expressive gin and plays gracefully with the orange garnish, the classic finishing flourish to traditional Negroni construction.

The final element of the Negroni's robust worldwide popularity is its relative ease of construction; nearly anyone can make a version of this drink at home, which is much to its benefit. The Negroni need not be subjected to a 30-step,

3-day centrifugal treatment—it is a drink for everyone. We hope you very much enjoy this drink, which at its heart is a reverently traditional spin on the Negroni format made all the better by the inclusion of coffee, not unlike life itself.

Step 1 of this recipe (making coffee ice cubes) is where some purists might start howling—"Won't that ruin the coffee?"—a topic upon which there is widely differing information online. The short answer is that for our purposes in cocktail creation, the end result is only ruinous if one Coffee Negroni

RECIPE CONTINUES

turns into three or four. Just be quick with the cube-to-shaker train of action, avoid storing coffee cubes in the fridge for weeks, and make a fresh batch a night or two before you intend to stir up your Negroni. Please also avoid the temptation to garnish this drink with coffee beans, which are a lovely addition to some but not all coffee cocktails.

Note: We've tweaked the classic 1:1:1 Negroni ratio with an eye toward the role our diluted coffee cubes will play. A soft touch with the vermouth is agreeable to this drink.

```
Makes 1 drink
Partners Coffee Honduras La Cueva, or your favorite coffee,
    brewed via Chemex, AeroPress, or your preferred brewing
    method, cooled to room temperature
1.5 ounces (3 tablespoons) Monkey 47 Schwarzwald Dry Gin
1 ounce (2 tablespoons) Punt e Mes vermouth
1.5 ounces (3 tablespoons) Campari
Orange peel, for garnish
```

1 —— **Pour the coffee into** square rocks molds (any old ice cube mold will do, but square is best) and place in the freezer.

2 —— **When the coffee ice** cubes are frozen (3 hours should do it, depending on your freezer), combine the gin, vermouth, and Campari in a shaker or pitcher with a single coffee cube. Stir 13 times clockwise in accordance with Japanese craft cocktail tradition.

3 —— **Add another coffee ice** cube to a lowball glass, then pour the gin mixture over it. Garnish with an orange peel and drink while considering the next steps of your evening.

A NOTE ON GIN: Germany's gin distilling scene is hot, and Monkey 47 Schwarzwald Dry Gin by Black Forest Distillers has become quite popular among bartenders. It is a notably savory gin, offsetting traditional gin aromatics like citrus peel and juniper with botanicals like cinnamon, cloves, licorice, and sage. This depth and complexity play quite well with coffee.

A NOTE ON VERMOUTH: Italy's Punt e Mes is a household name in the bar world, hailing from Torino. Our use of it here is a nod to the Fergroni, our personal favorite Negroni variation, as perfected by Fergus Henderson and the bar team at London's St. John restaurants.

CHARTREUSE CAPPUCCINO

The concept and recipe for this delicious beverage come courtesy of our friend Paul Einbund, whose restaurants in San Francisco—the Morris and Maison Nico—both serve the drink. We adore these places and cannot recommend them enough, but while you're there, you simply must try Paul's inspired creation: the Chartreuse Cappuccino.

Paul is a self-described "Chartreuse completist obsessive," and at the Morris they've got more than a hundred different bottles of the stuff, some dating back more than a century. Also a serious coffee aficionado, somewhere along the way Paul began experimenting with combinations of Chartreuse and espresso before finally hitting on this extraordinary expression.

"Espresso is rude and milk is forgiving," says Paul. "When you add a little bit of sugar and Chartreuse into the mix, that's when things get really interesting." Here's Paul's recipe for a remarkable Chartreuse Cappuccino, which to us evokes many happy memories of foggy nights in the City by the Bay and delicious mornings with pastries from Maison Nico.

Note: Paul Einbund's version of this drink makes use of yellow Chartreuse, resulting in a drink that's not visibly much different from a classic cappuccino. In our experiments in the lab, we leaned more toward using green Chartreuse, which offers a sweet, vegetal note to the drink that complements the espresso notes. To amplify the visual a bit more, try adding just a dash of matcha powder—perhaps 0.25 gram, or ¾ teaspoon—to the milk mixture before steaming (you will need an espresso machine's steam wand to make this drink), resulting in an altogether green and beautiful finished drink.

Makes 1 drink (8 ounces)

1 ounce (2 tablespoons) yellow or green Chartreuse (roughly three-quarters of a standard shot glass)

4 ounces (½ cup) whole milk or alternative milk of your choice

1 barspoon (1 teaspoon) palm sugar syrup (see Note on page 170)

¾ teaspoon of matcha powder (optional; see Note above)

1 espresso shot (1.5 ounces, 3 tablespoons, roughly equivalent to a double shot)

RECIPE CONTINUES

1 —— **Add the Chartreuse, milk,** palm sugar syrup, and the matcha powder (if using) to a steaming pitcher for milk. Steam the mixture together using the steam wand on your espresso machine. You're looking for traditional cappuccino foam here—frothy and not too wet. You will notice that the steamed milk is fragrant from the sugar and Chartreuse, which is very much the point.

2 —— **Pull a shot of** espresso into a shot glass or demitasse and pour it into a cappuccino cup or ceramic mug.

3 —— **Pour the steamed milk** mixture over the espresso in the style of a cappuccino and serve immediately.

A NOTE ON PALM SUGAR: This is typically found in the United States as an imported product from Southeast Asia. Paul Einbund recommends a type called Gula Melaka, which hails from Malaysia and has a deeply caramelized and smoky taste. Look for palm sugar at your favorite pan-Asian grocery store, or order it online. If that's not possible, demerara sugar, jaggery, or panela are all acceptable substitutes.

THE DUDE UBES

Sometimes a fun coffee cocktail starts out inspired by a single ingredient. Other times new drinks come into this world as riffs on cocktail history, loving variations on the cocktails that came before them. But no cocktail is a vacuum, and cultural inspiration is a great driver of creativity. The great drink at your favorite bar may have been inspired by a moment in a movie, perhaps, or the bartender's favorite song. These ideas aren't mutually exclusive—and here we have a drink that's something like a fusion of multiple ideas, resulting in something that perhaps was always meant to be. So goes the purple ube White Russian, which we're calling The Dude Ubes.

We are reasonably sure—not entirely sure but reasonably—that this is something like a drink of our own creation, fusing the round, profound flavors of purple ube yam with the singularly stochastic White Russian, a drink more or less apart from the classic cocktail tradition and yet undeniably a cocktail classic. We do know, for sure, that when you type the phrase "The Dude Ubes" into Google with quotes around it, there are exactly zero returns, so at the very least we're claiming the name.

Isn't ube wonderful? A sweet purple yam with a geographically protected heritage hailing from the Philippines, ube has a long culinary history and many expressions, from cheesecake to flan, pudding to halo-halo to jams, butters, and other spreads. Ube's popularity in America has grown considerably in recent years (that beautiful purple color sure helps), and today it represents that rarest of phenomena: a social media star with real substance behind it, deserving of all the praise and attention. We are particularly enamored with the use of ube at Hood Famous Bakeshop, a small Filipino bakery and coffee bar in Seattle's International District that makes riotously good ube cookies, mini ube cheesecakes, and a signature ube iced latte that is outrageously good. (Try substituting this syrup in place of chocolate in your next Caffe Mocha from page 102.)

The White Russian is a weird drink, most typically made with vodka, heavy dairy, and Kahlúa. When we talk about a White Russian, we are talking about three things: sweetness, milkiness, and coffee booze. Those three

RECIPE CONTINUES

elements can be supplied in a combination of ways; they do not require you to hew exactly to the traditional White Russian paradigm in order to create a drink of the tradition. With apologies to Jeffrey Lebowski, drinking any quantity of straight half-and-half is kind of gross; instead we are going to use some nice creamy oat milk via Pacific Foods. Your build looks as follows:

The sweetness—and a lovely shade of purple—comes courtesy of a full shot of Hood Famous Bakeshop's ube simple syrup, which sits beautifully with oat milk and coffee vodka. Yes, this will result in a sweet drink; it is supposed to be a sweet drink—this is required for it to feel like a member of the White Russian family. The coffee note comes not via a liqueur but rather by using some of our very own trusty homemade coffee vodka (see page 146). You are most definitely drinking a White Russian riff, but it does not look—or taste—like a White Russian. This is a good drink. The ube abides.

```
Makes 1 drink (4 ounces)
2 ounces (¼ cup) Incredibly Good Homemade Coffee Vodka (see
    page 146)
1 ounce (2 tablespoons) purple ube simple syrup
Ice rocks (enough to fill the bottom of your lowball glass—2
    or 3 medium cubes should do it)
A float of oat milk (preferably Pacific Foods) or nondairy milk
    of your choice
```

1 ——— **Combine the coffee vodka** and ube simple syrup over the ice rocks in a lowball glass. Swirl gently with a barspoon or chopstick to incorporate.

2 ——— **Pour the oat milk** over the top slowly. Perhaps have your camera ready, because the marble-swirl poetry of purple ube and creamy milk looks incredible in this moment.

In Conclusion: From the Coffeelands to Your Home

If you're anything like us, each morning you wake up, draw your first breath, and begin immediately thinking about that first cup of coffee. (We've been known to dream about it the night before.) Coffee takes us on a journey from the liminal state of rested waking to something more like terra firma, arming us with the cognition and inspiration to tackle that which lies ahead. It has been for generations the fuel that fires our engines each day, offering fortitude and pep in equal measure—Dolly Parton's "cup of ambition" making it possible for us to work that 9 to 5, wherever it may be, and whatever the actual hours are. (These days, work from home has changed everything *but* our coffee habits.)

We will forever cherish coffee for its stimulating effects, but in this book we've shown you how coffee can be so much more: it is not just a jolt of energy but rather a culinary multiuse tool capable of a broad diversity of expressions and inclusions, something that's beautiful not just on your kitchen counter but also in your refrigerator and home bar. Along the way, we've posed and answered the rhetorical question, **What are all the things you can do with a bag of delicious coffee?** It turns out that there are dozens of answers and counting—more and more to enjoy, in every way, at every step of life's journey.

But there is another journey we want to close by reflecting on, one that spans a good deal farther than just the distance between your refrigerator and your home bar cart. And this is the journey that coffee itself takes, from the farms and forests of the coffeelands to every corner of the globe. Whether they're in huge cities with millions of people or lonely islands serving a community of dozens, coffee shops and roasters are the next-to-last link in a global chain that stretches impossibly far and wide, impacting individual lives and the livelihoods of whole communities and nations. Coffee is one of the most global things we do each day, and an appreciation of that fact, we'd argue, is critical to understanding and enjoying coffee's true identity: more than a pick-me-up, more than an epicurean joy, it is in fact a marvel and triumph of human connectivity.

It's important to acknowledge the very real human beings at every step of this chain and the fact that they do not all come to it with the same equal footing. The amount earned by the coffee farmer for picking coffee is still, by and large, far too low; and the amount we pay for that coffee as consumers is also too low, particularly when you begin to appreciate the full possibilities of coffee as an agricultural product and culinary delight. Addressing these inequalities has become a major talking point in the coffee industry, and it is the focus of many worthwhile NGOs and fairly traded new business models. We are inspired by the work of roasters and importers in the Western world who voluntarily pay more already for coffee as a raw material and for a growing base of coffee lovers and consumers who understand that the old ways—of a bottomless $1 cup of coffee with free refills—are built, even if without knowing, on exploitation of labor by poor farmers on the other side of the planet. We don't say all this as a way of implying guilt or to make you feel bad about loving an affordable cup. The economics and ethics of coffee are complex, the subject of exhaustive book-length works written by historians and economists, and we have no interest in flattening these issues.

More than anything else, we want to leave you with a deeper appreciation and understanding of coffee—how to brew it, how to make delicious things with it, but also where it comes from, and your link in the chain—because you are a vital part of this: the last step in an international story that knits together the lives of people who might never otherwise meet but are nonetheless connected. Coffee has a possibility for global impact that makes it unique among the things we consume, and once you're armed with that knowledge, we hope it inspires you to think more deeply about who grows your coffee and how their lives can be bettered when the coffee trade acts fairly and equitably along every step of the chain.

The truth is some of the most interesting and beautiful coffees in the world right now are being grown, processed, roasted, and served all within a single country of origin; the import model we rely on in, say, the United States in many ways pales in comparison to the direct access to beautiful coffees enjoyed right now by coffee lovers in places like Colombia, Ethiopia, Kenya, and Indonesia, to name just a few countries with excellent domestic coffee scenes. Coffee's long, complicated, and at times painful history as an export crop, grown by farmers for pennies and sold to the West at a hefty profit is directly contradicted by similar kinds of developments, and these days our work at Sprudge is increasingly focused on incredible new coffee bars and roasting brands opening in Nairobi and Ho Chi Minh City, Oaxaca, and Vitória, and many more places across every corner of the coffee-growing world. Even this way of thinking about things—"producing" countries as opposed to "consuming" countries—is old-fashioned and rooted in colonialism. The way we think and talk about coffee in these contexts is changing very fast and, we'd argue, for the better, bringing more and more coffee lovers into the conversation and creating more and more expressions of coffee culture, influenced by different approaches to and appreciation of the beverage from all around the world.

Remember: this all started with a bag of delicious coffee. There are dozens of culinary paths that a single bag of coffee might take, and we have absolutely adored exploring them with you. But we really do want to implore you—beseech you—to think of coffee as being an intellectual matter every bit as much as a question of flavor or recipes. Coffee is a vast galaxy of history and meaning, and when you take this all in as a whole, the end result is breathtaking. Patronizing great roasters that work with reputable importers is part of this equation, but it's just the start. Mindfully enjoying your coffee to the fullest extent and allowing coffee to express itself as a gloriously multipurpose ingredient are ways to ultimately show respect to coffee's history and to the artisans who make that coffee possible from seed to cup. It's a delicious ingredient, yes, but it's also so much more. Learning about coffee, feeling inspired by and reverent toward coffee—it somehow makes it all taste better. It gives us a drink with meaning.

It's never been a better time to love coffee, to care about coffee, and to explore its possibilities as a springboard for good in the world. These are big ideas, we know—sounds like it's time to brew another cup.

Acknowledgments

Writing about coffee—thinking about coffee, drinking coffee, photographing coffee in its many forms and contexts, and sharing that love of coffee with the public—is a great joy and profound privilege for us. Any work on this topic would not be possible without the work of artisan coffee growers and capable trade professionals around the world. Many hands help guide coffee at every step of the way, from seed to cup. We want to thank everyone involved in this process from the bottom of our coffee-loving hearts.

Additionally, the authors would like to thank our loving and patient families, the brilliant and capable team at Sprudge, our tireless recipe testers, the careful stewardship and advocacy of Alison Fargis at Stonesong Press, and everyone at the team at Union Square & Co. for believing in us and extending the opportunity to create this book. Thank you for making coffee at home with us in all of its many forms.

Index

Note: Page references in *italics* indicate photographs.